Winning Compliance Auditing with Gung Fu Fighting Philosophy

Step by step guide for efficient, effective compliance audits instilled with a martial spirit

By Phillip H. Lee, CPA (Retired)

Library of Congress Control Number: 2022920293

To dad, for letting me spread my wings and fly from Fresno to Silicon Valley

Table of Contents

Why I am Writing This Book

The reason I am writing this book is I wish a book like this existed when I first started auditing for the federal government at the Defense Contract Agency (DCAA) in 1986. I received almost no formal training (one week in Memphis) in my first year and it took me several years to really get a good handle on what I was doing. I did not learn I was working on performance/compliance audits until I started at US Customs Regulatory Audit Division (RAD), 20+ years after my career began! I do not want the same fate to happen to anyone else to face the struggles and uncertainty of what to do on a compliance audit. The training I have received at both DCAA and RAD were usually quite specialized and related to specific topics. I would usually forget the information a few days after walking out of the classroom. There were no end-to-end training classes to explain the overall compliance audit process and how to be successful against the companies we were auditing.

In addition, there is a dearth of books on compliance auditing. The only literature I can find in public is in the GAO yellow book. Compliance audits are a type of performance audit in the GAO yellow book. Most if not all books out there are related to financial auditing. Very little emphasis is put on compliance auditing despite the fact that any government agency, public accounting firm, or private industry company performing compliance audits where the objective is to determine if an entity is complying with government regulations and quantifying loss of revenue can benefit from this book. There are probably at any point in time thousands, if not, tens of thousands of auditors performing compliance audits in this country and around the world.

Also, the compliance auditor is in an adversarial relationship with the auditee. In a compliance audit, you can go one on one with the auditee, like in a street fight. Therefore, I have incorporated martial arts and a "street" mentality/philosophy to help the compliance auditor defeat his adversary (auditee) pursing a winning methodology. I am not sure this has ever been attempted before, but I feel this idea has merit and could lead to more successful compliance audits.

Finally, my motivations for writing this book were born out of the struggles and hardships of trying to truly understand and excel at performing compliance audits without proper training and guidance. I was finally able to overcome all these obstacles and in the process was able to develop an approach or method for performing compliance audits, Plan, Organize, Execute, Reporting (POER). Sort of like how Tai Chi or Ba Qua was created. As a Chinese-American, I have found that it is quite difficult to get promoted in the federal government. I was always ignored and considered an average to below average auditor as management was oblivious to my achievements. They never understood or recognized my abilities. Rather than chase a hopeless dream of being recognized and promoted or quietly quitting, I have spent my time and energy developing my skills which have led to this book. I still have a giant chip on my shoulders!

I made a quantum leap in my skillset when an epiphany occurred to me in my 6th year at DCAA as my Supervisor at the time instructed me to look at another auditor's completed audit. I was blown away on how well organized his workpapers were and how he set up the audit using/following the audit program as the focal point. He also connected his audit together by referencing from the audit program to the workpapers and finally to the audit report. I then merged this auditor's organization method with my innate talent of performing risk assessments developed over years of performing hundreds of compliance audits and finding tens of millions of dollars of questioned costs at DCAA and Loss of revenue (LOR) at US Customs Regulatory Audit to create the Plan, Organize, Execute, Reporting (POER) methodology

With the burgeoning budget deficits in this country at both the local, state, and federal levels, it is more critical than ever that compliance auditors work as efficiently and effectively as possible in order to recover unreported government revenue and identify non-compliances with regulations. The compliance auditor should be at the vanguard of this movement to balance budgets to the extent possible by capturing unreported revenue and reporting non-compliances with government regulations. Compliance auditors are outgunned by the auditees due to stagnant or declining government budgets while companies in private industry have no such limitations on budget which puts compliance auditors at a huge disadvantage in resources and talent.

This is my attempt to level the playing field by coming up with a more martial and organized approach to compliance auditing based on my experiences in various martial arts and POER method which will result in more efficient and effective compliance audits. The beauty of my methodology is that it will not cost government agencies any more resources than what is in the gray matter between their ears. Sophisticated AI programs will only take government agencies so far without the proper perspective and thinking which I have tried to provide to the reader here.

The importance of compliance audits can't be underestimated. The recent increase in IRS's budget is one of the few ways the federal government can generate revenue. Increasing the effectiveness and efficiency of compliance audits at DCAA, US Customs Regulatory Audit, and other audit agencies performing compliance audits could potentially generate millions or billions in additional government revenue. As the federal government has been unable to cut spending or raise federal taxes in a meaningful way, this is one area where no additional resources need be allocated but additional government revenue could be generated.

I have also included some recommendations for property tax auditors based on my experience at DCAA and US Customs Regulatory Audit in Chapter 2. In addition, our country is also going through a Fentanyl crisis. Therefore, I have included a recommendation in Chapter 8, on utilizing US Customs Regulatory audit with the assistance of US Customs Port personnel, to take the lead or, assist other agencies, in combating trade-based money laundering, which helps fund this scourge, which has destroyed the lives of so many Americans. We must make eliminating trade-based money laundering a priority in this country as other disparate methods to stop it have not proved effective. We must cut off funding to these foreign scumbags in Mexico and China who would destroy our country with Fentanyl!

As our country is so divided right now. Asians are being targeted for robberies and violent assaults on the streets. As a Chinese American, I am trying to build a respect for Asian culture and thinking. I believe this book could be a bridge that will help relations between Asians and other Americans in this country. We need to unify this country and the first step is for all of us to respect each other cultures and thinking. As Asians seem strange and foreign to other Americans, Asians such as myself, need to bring Asian thought to the public; so that other races can understand us and know the cleverness and ingenuity of our culture.

Potential Users of this Book

Who can use this book to best effect

US Customs Regulatory auditors

DCAA auditors

State and Local property tax auditors

Federal, state, and local revenue audit agencies

Inspector General auditors (various agencies)

GAO auditors

General use of this book

Financial Auditors

Internal Auditors

Audit Training Coordinators

College/students looking to become compliance auditors

Medicare/Medical Auditors

Premium Insurance auditors

US Trustee (Bankruptcy) auditors

Federal Bureau of Investigation

Companies doing their own compliance audits

CPA consultants who specialize in Compliance Audits

College/University Auditors

This book is pretty unique as it is about performing compliance audits. There is a scarcity of information related to compliance audits, probably, because there is no central organization/agency in charge of performing compliance audits. Instead, separate federal, state, and local government agencies perform these audits with their own separate management, training and methodology of performing compliance audits. The author is attempting to introduce a novel strategy and plan of action to perform compliance audits with the main objectives of identifying non-compliance with government regulations and collecting unreported revenue. Although the author uses examples from DCAA and US Customs and makes recommendation for property tax audits, the author believes many of his concepts related to compliance audits can be carried over to other federal, state and local agencies performing compliance audits. In addition, both new and experienced auditors performing other types of audits can benefit from the general concepts of this book.

Introduction

It may seem strange that I am combining Gung fu fighting philosophy with compliance auditing. I believe the two have many common traits. In the Wikipedia Website, the definition of Gung fu is: '" Any study, learning, or practice that requires patience, energy, and time to complete." As in most trades/skills, to be successful in compliance auditing, you must study, learn, and practice (actually perform audits) in order to be really good at it. You also must take a martial attitude in order to be successful at compliance auditing. You must control your adversary and predict his moves. I mean this in an intellectual sense, in that based on your planning, organizing, executing, and reporting of the compliance audit, you will always stay one step ahead of the auditee. If you let the auditee control you, you will lose from the very beginning of the audit to the end. You must keep the auditee off-balance and unable to predict/determine your next move.

A well planned, organized, and executed audit will be difficult for any auditee to withstand. Do not contend with the auditee, instead, you must be willing to outwork, outhustle, outthink the adversary. That must be your goal to win at compliance auditing! This book is meant for college students or new graduates interested in pursuing a career in compliance audits, new compliance auditors coming into the industry of compliance auditing, as well as seasoned professional compliance auditors and audit management who might want to try a different approach to compliance auditing, training coordinators, and consultants, or even financial auditors who want to see things in a different perspective. Anyone who wants or needs a hardnose, practical guide on compliance auditing.

Compliance audits are covered in Generally Accepted Government Audit Standards (GAGAS) Yellow Book under Performance Audits (Chapter 1.22). Based on my research of the internet, very little if any books have been written on how to effectively perform a compliance audit. This is surprising considering how many government agencies are performing compliance auditing to determine if companies are complying with government regulation and paying proper amounts of revenues to the government (Chapter 1.25). Almost all books out there in the public are focused on financial accounting/auditing.

As a result, there is no coherent methodology to follow for compliance audits or much information available. Based on my experience, most agencies have their own specialized training courses and methods of performing compliance audits. I am attempting something different here as I am creating a book of a general approach to compliance auditing and introducing ideas on how to plan, organize, execute, and report a compliance audit using a martial attitude as the federal government, at least, holds almost unlimited power for IRS and US Customs, i.e., they can seize your real or personal property and auction if off. Or the government can take you to court on criminal or civil charges. Under criminal charges, you might have to pay three times the amount of loss of revenue (LOR). Therefore, auditors should approach these audits with the seriousness of a warrior in order to prevail on these audits. There are plenty of books on financial auditing as well as AICPA and loads of guidance. However, compliance auditing has remained in the shadows with little attention. In my career, I have found a method or way to perform this type of audit which I believe will lead to more successful audits. There is a martial and organized way of approaching these audits which I believe is missing in most training manuals.

I have 29 years of experience performing compliance audits and I also spent two years on the Quality Assurance (QA) team at US Customs Regulatory Audit, where I got to review audits performed around the country to determine if they complied with GAGAS standards. What I saw during my reviews was a lot of confusion and audits based on poor judgments which were also unorganized as well as poorly written audit reports. The experience at Quality Assurance helped me determine whether audits were performed in conformance with GAGAS and brought to a climax of my career as I finally understood the technical aspects of an audit as only a person who had done quality assurance audits could experience. I was able to find significant deficiencies in several audits I reviewed for the QA team and based on some of my findings, a training course was developed by US Customs Headquarters to correct some of the problems my findings exposed.

Because I received little to no training early in my career and it took me six years at DCAA to finally develop my method of performing compliance audits which I used for the last 25 years (18 years at US Customs) of my career to great success. I was able to survive at DCAA even when there was around 90% turnover due to firings, high cost of living, and difficulty of an auditing job with no training except for a week in Memphis. Although I was never promoted to management, I feel my skill in audit was above all other auditors. None could touch me in terms of audit results, as I was finally able to overcome the roadblocks thrown up by the companies I audited. I was auditing using a logical, objective, scientific method again and again to great success. I was always given the most difficult assignments at DCAA and US Customs Regulatory Audit that other auditors couldn't or wouldn't perform and was able to complete them better than the "crackerjack" auditors that management seemed to love, while using my method. As a result of using my method, I completed hundreds of compliance audits which resulted in cost savings to the federal government of tens of millions of dollars in the course of my 31-year career.

The reason my method is more effective is that I consider the other side and I am on the offensive, attacking the auditee from every angle keeping him off balance with an objective, scientific approach that is easy to understand and follow which results in devastating results to the auditee. Compliance audits are like a chess match in many ways. Really good chess players are always several moves ahead of their adversary. You must have this mindset as well as a street mentality (think like a criminal would on how to make money illegally).

Auditing is not a polite event like going to a picnic or party. It is more like a knife fight or going mano a mano to a street fight. The purpose is to rip the façade off the company you are auditing to expose all its secrets to maximizing profits by ripping off the government. In addition, my POER method connects all parts of the audit together, making the audit stronger. Knowing a lot of technical information and using artificial intelligence is only going to get you so far if you are not actively trying to stay ahead of your adversary on an intellectual level. I prefer good "old fashioned auditing" as my former boss at DCAA would say to me. Although at the time I didn't know what he was talking about. I think he meant that an auditor should use his/her "common sense".

This book is primarily relevant to Compliance audits and not financial audits as the objectives are different. My audits always related to complying with government regulations and quantifying any loss of revenue at DCAA and US Customs Regulatory Audit (RAD). The examples in this book are specifically related to audits performed at DCAA and RAD. However, some general aspects of my martial arts-oriented auditing may be applicable to other audits. It is my hope that some of the philosophy in the planning and risk assessment and organization of audit program, workpapers, and report could be utilized by financial auditors as well as other auditors.

My method is my personal method, and my opinions and priorities are my own. This is what has worked for me as an auditor and take from this book what you will. But always follow what your organization/Agency tells you to do and focus your time on. Hopefully, this will help some auditors who come to the same conclusions as I do on how to be the most effective auditor in a government agency where you are outgunned by the auditee, consultants, attorneys, and experts. The compliance auditor must work in the most efficient, cost effective, smart way in order to stay ahead with little guidance or support in many instances. Your supervisor/manager may have limited experience in audit and/or rely on prior audits and training from headquarters. I am offering a different perspective based on 29 plus years performing difficult audits without any help.

All of the steps in a compliance audit are connected in that parts of each flow down starting from the audit program and planning steps to the next steps in the compliance audit until all steps are connected together in the workpapers and report writing.

This book does not answer every question or situation about auditing and may not apply to all compliance audits. Again, this book covers mainly US Customs and DCAA audits. But you can apply the general techniques and ideas based on this book to your particular situation. (See my recommendations on property tax auditors in Chapter 2). I am writing this book in the hopes that if an auditor is not given proper training like in my situation, this book could help future auditors from avoiding the mistakes and pain I went through to learn things the "hard way" by performing hundreds of audits for 29 years.

I end this Introduction with some thoughts on artificial intelligence (AI). I have recently used ChatGPT-4 and I believe this is going to drastically change the audit profession. Writing and answering emails, creating presentations, writing training manuals, can all be done almost instantly with the right prompt engineering. However, I believe that, artificial intelligence cannot replace a person's spirit or create a new way to do things. AI can only predict based on its database. Federal agencies need to utilize artificial intelligence to the maximum extent possible as I believe this is the future of auditing and it may someday make this profession a lot easier! I used ChatGPT-4 one time in this book to obtain import data for 2020. I believe most books written in the future will be created by artificial intelligence and that is a shame. New ideas still need a place! I feel I am bringing a fresh perspective to compliance auditing with this book. Humans still need to create new ideas in order to survive in the coming years or we will eventually be replaced by robots! For instance, my recommendation to US Customs Regulatory Audit and US Customs Port personnel to become more involved or take the lead in combating trade-based money laundering in order to fight the scourge of Fentanyl in our country exported from

China and Mexico is included in Chapter 8. This is a novel thought that I created and something artificial intelligence cannot accomplish yet. I envision a world where humans create better ways to solve the world's problems and use artificial intelligence as a helper/servant to aid in this great endeavor.

Chapter 1
Defining Objective of Compliance Audit

In compliance audits the first thing you have to do is to determine what your objective is. The overall objective of most compliance audits is: To determine if the company is complying with the relevant government regulations for your agency and to determine if there is any loss of revenue/taxes owed. You can usually determine your objective by determining whether your audit was initiated in the government database system by selection for audit based on certain criteria or because of a request from another government department or Agency.

If you start your compliance audit without a proper objective, you are like a ship without a rudder. I was eye witness to a story about an auditor at Defense Contract Audit Agency (DCAA) which became a legend of sorts. In the Bay Area Field Office, I was assigned to after getting a job at DCAA. There was an auditor named W. G. who was fired at the 9 month point in his career as this is before the 12 month point where an employee attains permanent status as a government employee. This was not an unusual event at DCAA, as there was 90 to 100 percent turnover during my first three years at DCAA due to the difficulty of doing audits without training once you went through the door of the office and the incredibly high cost of living in the Bay Area in 1986-1987. Auditors would be given several audits with short turnaround times and expected to put together audits without any training. The Supervisory Auditors would write down short instructions and tell the auditors to go look at prior audits completed. But since many of the prior audits were performed by auditors who were no longer there, you could never be sure you were working with anything approaching a quality audit.

Anyhow, W. G. was struggling and was given a proposal audit, which involves reviewing direct and indirect costs proposed for a government contract. There are direct costs and indirect costs involved, which involved labor rates, labor hours, direct costs, Overhead, and G&A, etc. The only formal training W. G. received was a one-week course in Memphis. As a result of this, W. G. had no clue what to do on his audit, so he apparently focused on reconciling FICA taxes to the general ledger. The FICA taxes would be part of fringe benefit costs which would have been allocated to Direct Labor, overhead labor and G&A labor allocated based on total labor costs. Poor W. G. was sent out to perform a compliance audit without knowing the objective and the result was that he ended up doing a payroll audit of Social Security tax, which is only a small and insignificant portion of what he was supposed to do. Besides the fact that IRS and state agencies are responsible for these taxes and not DCAA.

I used to watch W. G. as I started just before he got fired and attended his going away lunch. Another auditor gave his going away speech and slammed DCAA's management for lack of training and the poor pay in such an expensive area. I remember all the management walking out in the middle of the speech. This incident left a huge impression on me and I swore to myself I would not end up like this. Well, I received the bare minimum score for promotion on my annual appraisal minimum to pass promotion. Anything less and I would have been put on a 3 months performance improvement plan and eventually fired.

How do you know what the true objective is: In a compliance audit, the rule is to follow the money! The overall objective of a compliance audit is to determine if the company is complying with the government regulations and calculate any revenue lost. The revenue lost part is where you follow the money!

I will explain in detail follow the money in the next chapters on planning risk assessment. But suffice it to say that you must understand the auditee's motivations and ways that it can circumvent the government regulations in order to increase profits by getting extra funds from the government. The simplest ways to do this are by underpaying taxes or over estimating proposed and incurred cost submissions. This is not as simple as it sounds and it takes a lot of planning, preparation, and street smarts in order to fight a mental battle with the adversary (auditee), many of whom are very good at obfuscation and hiding things they don't want the government to know about.

This is why I have incorporated martial arts philosophy into the compliance auditing process so that the auditor will have a more level playing field. Right now, compliance auditors are at an extreme disadvantage to the companies they are auditing as the government is facing record deficits and there is a shortage of experience, competent compliance auditors at government agencies, while the companies being audited have unlimited resources in many cases and can hire outside attorneys and CPA firms to assist them. The only way to catch up to the companies being audited is to match them intellectually. That is why I am advocating using martial arts philosophy to help compliance auditors out think, out hustle, and out point the adversary they are auditing. The compliance auditor must be able to identify and attack the auditee's weak points, understand the government regulations, predict the adversary's response and counter attack if need be. The compliance auditor must audit in a scientific, objective way and go north south in the most direct, efficient way. The key is not only understanding the game but trying to master the game. Like chess the compliance auditor should try to be five steps ahead of the adversary. You must be able to completely focus on the audit objective from the beginning to the end of the audit in order to succeed. Lose focus and you will surely not succeed. You must be disciplined like a martial arts master!

If the audit was requested read the request carefully and determine exactly what the customer wants. Be sure to only perform audit procedures related to government related costs as sometimes requestors will ask us to audit non-government related costs which would veer the audit towards a fraud audit/review as the overall objective must go back to the government regulations. On self-initiated audits, I usually research the specific government regulations, headquarters guidance, audit programs, prior audits, etc. to get a sense of what needs to be done to accomplish the objective. Whether, there is a request or if it is self- initiated, a full audit or an agreed upon procedures, only do what the requestor asks for. For instance, if it is an agreed upon procedure, then no scope creep to a full audit! You should almost have a singular focus on what you're supposed to do. Give the customer what they want.

I would like to discuss the objective of finding non-compliances with government regulations and Loss of Revenue (LOR). They go arm in arm finding non-compliances with government regulations is just as important as finding LOR and in many cases are a result of LOR as the auditee is intentionally not complying with the regulation in many cases in order to get around paying LOR. In cases where the auditee's LOR is the cause of the noncompliance, that is the worst-case scenario and the riskiest for the compliance auditor. In cases where the company is just making errors causing the non-compliances and in cases where there is an overpayment of revenue due to errors, the compliance auditor should inform the auditee and the revenue should be refunded to comply with government regulations. However, these innocent non-compliance errors should not be the focus of the compliance auditor. They are far less relevant than the audit situations where the auditee is playing around with the regulations in order to increase profits. Government agencies lifeblood is Loss of Revenue (LOR). Loss of Revenue findings increase prestige for the agencies and now with the huge budget deficits being run by local, state, and federal agencies are becoming more important by the day.

Agencies can better their chances exponentially of getting budget increases if they come up with significant LOR at large companies. This also causes fear at the companies being audited, so the companies may submit disclosures and do their own self-audits and pay the government so that we don't audit them. The importance of identifying significant LOR in audits can't be understated and is very important sometimes to the very existence of compliance auditors. Given this importance, it is time that government agencies stop living on an island and start communicating with each other in relation to compliance audits. Identifying non-compliances and quantifying any LOR should be a standard used by government agencies performing compliance audits. This should be standardized somehow so that all local, state, and federal agencies collecting taxes/duties or involved in contract pricing estimates/incurred costs include non-compliances and LOR as part a standard for compliance audits. Make no mistake about the importance of LOR. Many tax agencies such as US Customs and IRS have the ability to seize assets and auction them for non-payment of taxes. This represents almost unlimited powers by government. It is time to put the importance of this into perspective especially given the financial straits we are in.

My hope is that someday this disparate group of compliance auditors can come together and come up with common standards/checklists utilizing GAGAS and work together to improve each other's agency planning, organizing, executing, and reporting. I hope that this book provides a start to this in the expectation that in the future, if compliance auditors were to work together to improve each other's procedures and reporting, this could greatly improve the compliance audits by banding together.

Perhaps starting an organization like financial auditors with compliance auditors from various agencies forming an AICPA or PCAOB type organization to set and improve standards and reporting to other government agencies. Compliance auditors can also solicit information from customers and other interested parties on what they want in terms of improvements and responsiveness to their requests. There should also be coordination between training at the various compliance auditing organizations to aid in setting up standards in order to improve and comply with GAGAS. I would like compliance auditors who read this book to send me their ideas on how to improve compliance especially agencies outside DCAA and US Customs. I would love to revise my book to include improvements to compliance audits at the federal, state, and local level. I am particularly interested in Loss of

Revenue potential as I feel this is the key to getting compliance auditing on the map in terms of publicity and marketing.

I would also be willing to set up a website on compliance auditing so that compliance auditors can brainstorm about ways to improve compliance audits at their agencies. We need to start a crusade to recover the millions or even billions of dollars out there that can help finance this great country.

Chapter 2A

Planning-Initial Preparatory Steps to Planning

In terms of audit, the main point on this is after you determine the objective, use all available information in order to plan your audit.

Beginning step: Audit Program

Attention: Start your audit here! Usually there is an audit program created by your headquarters in your government agency which is usually located in a database or MS Word or Excel files. Make sure you get the most current audit program. Audit programs are revised periodically and I have found audits at DCAA that were using outdated audit programs. Look at the date of the audit program and make sure it is the most current version. Carefully and purposely review every step in the audit program before beginning the audit. I call the audit program, the fulcrum, because it is the base/foundation of an audit. The auditor selects the subject areas to review. It is a central part of the planning process as it tells the reviewer/supervisory auditor exactly what you are going to do on the audit. The audit program flows down to everything in your compliance audit and is the central document which emanates through to every other workpaper in your audit. On the audit program you will reference to every workpaper and the audit report through a reference number which is located in a column located on the right side of the audit program page. Also, ensure that your supervisor signs and approves the audit program.

Never underestimate the power of the audit program. I remember an assignment at DCAA where I learned the importance of the audit program. I was assigned a Cost Accounting Standard /(CAS 414) audit which relates to Facilities Capital Cost of Money. Another senior auditor had the assignment but she sat on it for months as it was a self-initiated assignment with a due date a few weeks away. Anyway, when I received the assignment from her, I checked her workpapers and she gave me an empty binder with some DCAA forms that she had filled out. I looked in the files and no one had put out a Cost Accounting Standard (CAS 414) audit, so there was no example for me to follow. My supervisor was a strange person whose prior occupation was repossessing cars! I kid you not! She had transferred from Headquarters without ever performing an audit. Luckily, I was able to find the most recent audit program for the CAS 414 audit and fortunately for me, it was extremely detailed. Basically, it required me to verify net book value balances for selected asset categories at the beginning and end of the year. I then needed to verify the interest rate and allocation bases (overhead and G&A) were from valid sources. I remember putting the relevant paper documents all over the floor of my cubicle and organizing the audit from the ground up! I was able to reconcile the company's submission to its accounting records and interest rate to the required Federal interest rate in effect at the time. I accomplished in a week what would have taken this auditor an unknown amount of time to finish if she ever could have finished. Without knowing anything about the subject and having no prior audits to refer to, I was able to connect the dots and perform a rather difficult audit fairly easily and efficiently. This reinforced my respect and reverence for the audit program. Having good detailed audit programs is a tremendous asset!

A lot of audit programs are "pro forma" bare bones. This means the auditor must fill in the specific details of what to do. You must revise the audit program and use it as a "living" document which you can feel free to edit based on additional information derived from the risk assessment, information from interviews, questionnaires, checklists, etc.

An audit program is usually divided into sections:

Objective
Planning and Preparation
Internal Controls
Review Submission/Trade area/Proposal
Audit Testing – Evaluation of sample
Audit Closure – Summarize workpapers, Finalize Audit Report

Again, I always start with the audit program as the beginning document to review and understand what is going to be required to complete the audit. In rare cases where there is no audit program, you can create one yourself by reviewing the government regulation requirements and adding planning and audit report steps, etc. You can then perform a risk assessment to determine areas to review as well as Loss of Revenue potential to fill in the audit steps. You can copy from another audit program to get general steps and add in for preparation steps and audit report. Add internal control (I/C) review if required. After obtaining the audit program, here is list of documents for initial preparatory steps:

Review the following for initial preparatory steps:

Critical Document – Audit Program. Warning: Use most current version

Important Documents:

Government regulations for areas of review, 19 CFR (US Customs), FAR Part 31.205 (DCAA)

Audit Request to determine what customer wants done and why or if self-initiated audit, reason for selection

Supervisory Guidance related to audit areas to be reviewed

Headquarters Guidance related to audit areas to be reviewed

Audit information on your government agency websites such as Defense Contract Audit Agency, US Customs Regulatory Audit, State of California State Board of Equalization. Just do a Google search.

I also recommend U.S. Customs Broker License Examination Preparation Guide by Yuri Starikov, LLC available on Amazon. Excellent breakdown of trade areas with questions and answers which provide a wealth of information. US Customs should have one copy in each office for auditors. Any government agency that has a test should have these review materials available as training guides for auditors. I also recommend CPA firms keep copies of Becker CPA review or other CPA review courses so that auditors can refer to these materials.

Company financial statements, trial balance, BOD Minutes, etc. These documents should be kept in a permanent file for auditees

Government databases such as ACE for US Customs, AES for exports. Identify high risk trade areas such as Anti-Dumping duties. (US Customs), RAMIS to identify open and closed assignments for contractors (DCAA)
Government trade area checklists, Internal Control checklists, interviews with company

Company declarations, proposal, submissions. Note any irregularities such as Non-deductible costs being deducted from value, etc. (US Customs), company contract mix can sometimes be derived from incurred cost submission, identify unallowable costs excluded from indirect rates and composition of allocation bases (DCAA)

Horizontal/Vertical analysis current and prior years data to identify trends, variances

Information from the requesting government agency related to any problems found at the auditee

Agency training manuals – I use to attend a lot of classes at US Customs Regulatory Audit, but right after the class, I would put the three-inch binders in my cubicle and forget about it. Actually, these training manuals are a great reference/resource for specific audit areas for review. They usually include examples of situations you run across as well as recommendations on how to approach these risk areas. I highly recommend you review these on a regular basis.

Cost impacts, Disclosures of errors by the company. This is usually a red flag and indicates more audit effort may be required.

Agency manuals DCAA Contract audit manual, Focused assessment Manual – Another treasure trove of information. Refer to agency manuals as they usually show the regulations applicable to audit areas of review as well as audit approach to utilize.

Audit leads by other auditors

Tax returns (if available or under audit)

Information about company on the internet, physical observations, plant tours, etc...
Prior audits, non- compliances by the company which have not been resolved.

Be careful relying too much on prior audits, if they do not follow my POER methodology, they might not be very good. But certainly, if there are findings in the prior audits **agreed to by the company**, that would indicate if there are potential problems with the company and raise questions about the control environment of management.

At this initial point of the compliance audit process, you are just trying to get a general idea of what to do, so don't stress just yet. Try to understand the business you are auditing, get a general idea of major potential areas for review. Carefully read the regulations and headquarters guidance to get an understanding of where the emphasis of the audit should be in terms of risk and where the auditee could possibly take advantage (i.e. follow the money). If there are disclosures by the company and/or non-compliances noted, IMHO, we should not concentrate our review on the areas disclosed (just verify these) but I usually concentrate on areas in the disclosure where the company may not have disclosed any additional loss of revenue. The reason being, it is less likely you will come up with additional findings on disclosed areas which include LOR versus auditing "virgin areas" that the company did not include LOR for. Hit them where it hurts and always go for the jugular which is a large loss of revenue/money!!! Think of loss of revenue as the motherlode. Non-compliances and errors are nice but what distinguishes a true audit master is the one who can hit the company's checkbook hard. That is the crucible of what a compliance auditor should truly strive for.

In the Planning stage, identify/select large amount transactions and/or balances for review as you perform any analytical procedures. However, this step is preliminary and the concept of materiality should be detailed in the risk assessment.

Walkthrough with the Company

The next step is to schedule an entrance conference to meet with the company representatives. I usually use this opportunity to get more information from the company to identify risk areas. I write up an agenda and follow it during the entrance conference.

During the entrance conference or the first few days you are at the company, this is your chance to obtain documents and have any initial questions you had in the planning process answered by the company. You can also get more information to put into your risk assessment. The best information you can get is in writing. Oral information must be corroborated and usually the company will deny something they said to the auditor orally if asked. Best way is to get information in writing and corroborate by getting source documents to support what the company is saying. Try thinking like a scientist performing an experiment. You must have the proof to support your experiment's conclusion!

Gather together all the information you are going to go over with the company in the agenda which may include:

I. Introductions
II. Go over audit program
III. Walkthroughs – usually step in audit program
IV. Interviews – could be step in audit program
V. Questionnaires- could be in audit program or guidance
VI. Prior audits
VII. Disclosure by company
VIII. Questions regarding financial statement/tax returns/on-line information/High risk areas such as Anti-dumping

At this point, depending on the audit you could also review internal controls, but usually you will make another separate appointment for this as there are usually separate questionnaires, checklists, etc. that must be filled out (see below).

I go over the audit program with the company at the entrance conference as I am completely open with them on what I plan to do. This comes with the confidence that I will control them and I will always be honest and open with them and everything I obtain from them will be obtained legally and will be treated as sensitive information. I never withhold information from them and am always honest when I think I have a finding. I communicate the potential finding to the auditee right away. The worst thing you can do is wait until the end of an audit and find that what you thought you had found was a mirage. The company proves you wrong and you have egg foo young all over your face and lose all credibility. As an auditor/martial artist, you must always have honor and behave honorably. Don't be sneaky and dishonest. All a compliance auditor really has is credibility and without that, your really don't have anything.

Right from the beginning, I take a martial attitude. The questionnaire, checklists, and interviews will give you a chance to ask questions about preliminary areas you may be interested at this time which may go into the risk assessment and audit program if it turns out information you receive indicates potential! You can perform analytical horizontal and vertical procedures and bombs away ask all the questions you want about any unusual variances/differences.

When you perform your walkthrough, you basically document the document flow of transactions for the areas you were requested to audit or for self-initiated audits any areas you find to be of potential interest.

Usually this will give you valuable information about the documents the company utilizes, purchase orders, invoices, payments, etc. and will also give you an idea of the internal controls the company has in the various departments. You will also get specific internal control information during the internal control review, but this initial review will give you an idea of the complexity of the organization and the staffing. Use of flowcharts are very useful showing document flows and the type of personnel involved.

Perform walkthroughs, interviews, questionnaire, Review disclosure statements/Cost impacts, prior audits, company proposals, submissions, non-compliances, tax returns (if available), on-line information about company, etc., internal control review, checklists analytical procedures.

Internal Control Review

Internal Control review can be performed in conjunction with the entrance conference. In terms of Internal Control review, here is a summary of the steps performed.:

Internal Control review is required by GAGAS. It was developed by the COSO commission.

Fill out internal control checklist – The checklist usually covers the five main areas of internal control: Control environment, monitoring, risk assessment, information and communication, control activities

Usually, document walkthrough and create flowcharts of internal controls of areas of review.

Review written internal control procedures

Perform Interviews of relevant personnel

Document flow of transactions.

I have included separate chapters on internal control review and risk assessment.

Requests/Communication with the Company.

It is very important that the compliance auditor communicate with the auditee throughout the audit. It is a good idea to put your requests from the company in writing. This serves several purposes. Requests in writing can't be denied to exist by the company as verbal requests can often be. Also, if there are a lot of requests, you can keep track of the requests and if a response from the company is late, it is easy to identify on the request worksheet. You should number your requests and write up a worksheet which you can keep in the administrative section of your workpapers. An example of Request worksheet:

Request No.	Subject/Trade Area	Date Requested	Date Received
1	Financial statements Tax returns, G/L Trial Balance, BOD Meetings	2/1/xxxx	3/3/xxxx
2	Internal control policies And procedures	2/8/xxxx	3/13/xxxx
X	XXXXXXXXXXXX	XXXXXXXXXXXX	XXXXXXXXXXXX

Chapter 2B
Risk Assessment

Generally, the main thing to remember in risk assessment is: Follow the money! Just like in the objective, this will lead you to the gold at the end of the rainbow. Following the money will lead you to Loss of Revenue (LOR) which leads to non-compliance. How do you follow the money? Think of all the ways the auditee can get out of paying government taxes and that will go a long way towards your goal. I can't stress this enough. There is nothing closer to a brick wall than a bank statement in terms of strong evidence as payments in a bank statement are very difficult to excuse away as an error because it involves who/where the money is paid to! If you learn nothing else except follow the money and audit program, I will have achieved my goal of educating the audit community about compliance audits.

If the audit program is the fulcrum/foundation of the compliance audit, the risk assessment is the blood of the compliance audit. In a way, it is a living thing as keeps the heart and other vital organs alive and flows through the whole body. The risk assessment is flexible and can change based on the audit leads/information you obtain during the audit. In a fight, what do you do? Stand there in a fixed position and you will get clocked. Move out of the way at angles that are beneficial to your defense, then use your training to counter-attack. The risk assessment also flows and is connected to your audit program, workpapers and audit report. These concepts/documents are that important! When I talk about follow the money, I am referring to payments in relation to Compliance audits. Payments to vendors, employees, related parties, and others are part of price paid or payable to US Customs and make up incurred costs to DCAA.

If you follow the principle of look where they don't want you to look (usually the company's pocketbook), you will be on your way to a better compliance audit! Although most auditors are upright people who have studied hard in school and done all the right things in life; You must learn to think like the adversary. How do I misclassify/miscode an expense, obfuscate payments so not all costs included in price, put the wrong country of origin, include unallowable costs in a non-conspicuous account, miscode lease costs to a different nomenclature account. If there is a tax involved undervalue the tax rate and/or base. If it is a proposal/FPRA/Incurred cost overvalue by including extra unallowable/un-allocable, unreasonable costs. Basically; undervalue for tax purposes and overvalue to increase profits like on FFP/CPFF contract proposals/FPRA. Think sleazy but audit honestly.

The company must hide these manipulations through miscoding, misclassification, obfuscation and other means. You must play chess at the highest level and outthink your adversary to have any chance of success because the sad truth is the auditor has very limited resources while the companies have pretty much unlimited resources. You must work smarter not harder! I will now present to you the concepts of reported and unreported value in Compliance Audits. As auditors, we have to get rid of platitudes and phony excuses of why we are auditing at these companies. We are auditing to find Loss of Revenue and non-compliances! The worst case is when the auditee circumvents or manipulates government regulations to pay less tax or overestimate proposals/submissions. We are trying to rip the mask off the face of the company we are auditing!

Compliance audits are essentially adversarial in nature. GAGAS requirements ensure there are no conflicts of interest. This is in stark contrast to a financial audit which are somewhat compromised because the CPA firms performing the financial audits solicit and are also hired on by the same companies they are auditing for lucrative consulting and tax work. The financial auditor is trying to determine if the financial statements are presented fairly according to Generally Accepted Accounting Principles (GAAP). The financial auditor is not trying to find loss of revenue and non-compliance which can cause a lot of real conflict (fighting) with the auditee. The compliance auditor is unfettered by such restrictions and can play to win! Strike first and hard! Move before the adversary moves. Out think, out work, and out maneuver the adversary.

In order to perform a proper risk assessment, a compliance auditor must have a good understanding of the concepts of reported/unreported value as well as other important considerations, Therefore, I am going to summarize the organization of the rest of this chapter by section as follows: Sections I defines the meaning of reported and unreported value in compliance audits, Sections II justifies and explains my focus on unreported value in compliance audits. I then provide specific explanation/analysis of unreported value in US Customs and DCAA compliance audits. Section III are specific risk assessments for US Customs and DCAA compliance audits. Section IV are my recommendations on risk assessments for state and local property tax audits based on my experience at DCAA and US Customs, Section V explains materiality in compliance audits. Section VI covers fraud assessments. Section VII provides information on citing government regulations in compliance audits, Section VIII covers some other risk assessment considerations in compliance audits

Section

I. I explain the concept reported value and unreported value in compliance audits,

II. Justifies and explains my focus on unreported value in compliance audits. I then provide specific explanation/analysis of unreported value in US Customs and DCAA compliance audits

III. Risk Assessments for US Customs and DCAA compliance audits

IV. Recommendations to perform vendor payment analysis on Property Tax Audits and other procedures based on DCAA and US Customs experience

V. Materiality in compliance audits

VI. Fraud assessment

VII. Cite the Specific Government Regulation in compliance audits

VIII. Some other things to consider on your risk assessment

Section I
Reported Value and Unreported Value in Compliance Audits

Reported value and unreported value are intertwined together so I will attempt to explain the two together. It is difficult to explain one concept without explaining the other at the same time. Reported value and unreported value are like an action and reaction. You have to understand what reported value is so that you can determine what the unreported value is. Therefore, they are difficult to separate.

Reported value is what is reported to the government on a proposal or incurred submission at DCAA; What is declared to US Customs through the ACE system; Or what is stated on a property tax return. This is what is known and disclosed to the government. These are the amounts that are verified by reviewing the company's proposals, incurred cost submission, tax return, Customs declarations, FPRA, etc. and source documents such as general ledger/trial balance, purchase orders, invoices, packing list, Bill of lading, contracts between related parties, payments, bank statements, etc.

Unreported value represents transactions that are not disclosed by the auditee and therefore, hidden from the auditor which I believe should be an area of major focus in compliance audits. I discuss unreported value as a greater area of focus in Section II.

US Customs Regulatory Audit Reported/Unreported Value

For US Customs reported/unreported value, the important points are to first determine what the company is declaring as higher risk tariff items such as: Dutiable items, ADD/CVD and all other categories where good amounts of duties and fees were paid to the government due to high duties/fees. Then when you know that, look at areas that may not have been reported (declared) correctly such as non-dutiable imports, Special Programs, FTA, drawback etc. Focus on non-dutiable or lower duty items. Based on martial arts philosophy: Study the adversary. Identify his strengths and weaknesses. Reported (Declared) value exposes a company's strength and weakness. The importer's strength are the imports declared with high duties and fees, ADD/CVD, etc. The importer's potential weakness are imports declared as non-dutiable, FTA, Special Program, drawback. These imports are where the company could exploit the system and not pay the proper amounts of duties and fees.

In terms of US Customs, unreported values are also related to the auditee misclassifying imported merchandise to a lower duty rate, making additional payments or paying off the seller's debt, deducting non dutiable Costs (NDC) from declared value (estimated freight costs), excluding above market interest paid to seller, providing assists to the seller, claiming FTA, Drawback, Special Programs, etc. and falsifying documentation, not declaring ADD/CVD by misclassification and or undervaluation. Basically, undervaluing imported merchandise, misclassifying imported merchandise, or claiming special status when the imported merchandise does not qualify.

DCAA Reported/Unreported Value

DCAA's reported value are proposals/FPRA, incurred cost submissions. In the proposal/FPRA and incurred cost submissions, the auditee discloses direct costs, indirect costs, and fee/profit. Direct costs are made up of direct labor and direct material. Indirect costs are usually made up of overhead and G&A rates. The direct costs are charged directly to contracts and indirect costs are allocated to contracts based on allocation bases to contracts. This opens up a can of worms as both direct and indirect costs are subject to government regulations related to allowability, allocability, and reasonableness. The direct costs are proposed and incurred by contract through direct charging through timecards, purchase orders, invoices, payments for direct materials. Indirect costs are allocated to contracts through the use of overhead and G&A rates which are allocated through the use of allocation base Direct Labor + IR&D Direct Labor and Total Cost Input, respectively. There are relevant government regulations for these costs Federal Acquisition Regulations (FAR) 31.201 to FAR

31.205. The costs charged to government contracts must be allowable, allocable, and reasonable. The auditees propose costs on future contracts on proposals and incur costs which they submit as incurred cost submissions when the contracts are completed. There are different types of government contracts. FFP contracts which are based on a fixed negotiated price including profit, which is almost impossible to change except for acts of God, etc. under an equitable adjustment. Cost overruns on FFP contracts are not reimbursed which makes them risky. Cost type contracts are like the name says based on costs incurred plus a fee. The company will get paid for whatever costs they incur plus a fee. If they overrun the contract, they can ask for and usually get, with proper justification, a budget increase.

Reported values are direct labor and direct material cost, Overhead costs excluding unallowable and unreasonable costs, G&A costs excluding unallowable and unreasonable costs.

Unreported values are a little more complicated to explain. Because of the allocation between FFP and CPFF contracts, costs can be misallocated between these two types of contracts i.e. FFP to CPFF contracts or risky contracts to low-risk contracts. There is even more risk if there are commercial contracts as the company could try to shift commercial costs to CPFF contracts as well. In terms of unallowable and unreasonable costs. The auditor must review the auditee's general ledger/trial balance to identify unallowable and unreasonable costs that the company has not excluded from Fringes, Overhead and G&A and direct costs. The company will usually miscode the unallowable and unreasonable costs to other more innocuous accounts that the compliance auditor generally wouldn't suspect or look. I have put a lot of my personal experiences in more details below in the risk assessment section.

State/Local Property Reported/Unreported Value

I want to stress I do not have any experience in this area. But I believe I can make a recommendation here in terms of reported and unreported value based on my experience at US Customs Regulatory audit and DCAA. Reported value is what is stated as the value of assets on the property tax form times the property tax rate for commercial properties. These are usually audited by Local governments and regulated by State government. My recommendation is that auditors performing property tax audits should consider performing vendor analyses (unreported value) and other procedures to identify transactions in the General Ledger/Trial balance that are not coded correctly to possibly identify CIP, Leases, etc. that were not properly classified and/or reported on the property tax return. This idea is taken directly from my experience at US Customs and I believe it could be useful here as a lot of emphasis seems to be on verifying reported value.

I provide more details on the concept of unreported value in Section II. Specific risk assessments for US Customs, DCAA, and state and local tax agencies are in Section III and IV.

Section II
Justification and Explanation of my focus on Unreported Value in Compliance Audits with specific explanation/analysis of Unreported Value for US Customs and DCAA Compliance audits

I equate unreported value with completeness. How does the auditor know that the company they are auditing is including everything that should be included according to government regulation? The concept of completeness is important as this is behind the idea of unreported value and is the reason why I feel unreported value is so important and an area that is not always covered in compliance audits.

I consider this one of the black holes of compliance audit. Most compliance auditors concentrate their audit work on reported value because it is easy to audit the information that the company puts in front of your face. It is exponentially more difficult to go after a company for unreported value. This requires a lot of creativity and imagination from the compliance auditor as well as some street smarts. The compliance auditor must have a clear focus on the audit objective, be able to follow the money and sniff out the obfuscations and misclassifications put out by the auditee to prevent the compliance auditor from finding their "profit" or "ill-gotten gains". It takes a lot of moxie from the compliance auditor to take on an adversary on such a high intellectual level, like a chess game. The compliance auditor must know what he is doing to stay several steps ahead of the adversary.

In the government, no one in management will question you if you decide not to look at unreported value, especially if it is not included in the audit program and headquarters guidance and training. However, based on my 29 years of performing compliance audits, I believe you are missing out on potentially huge amounts of loss of revenue and non-compliances. In order to truly know if the auditee is being honest and compliant with the government, a review of unreported value must be performed!

I would like to expound of why I think unreported value is a valuable concept. This is a concept I formally developed mostly from US Customs, Although, I probably was informally using this concept at DCAA. Basically, this theory involves reviewing what the auditee had reported or made known to the auditor and basically looking for weaknesses in other transactions that are not known to the auditor by evaluating where the auditee is going to make bank on whatever obfuscation, the company is using to increase profits! Think of ways a company can jerk off the government, hide it, and get away with it and you will be way ahead of other auditors. The company's strength is where they have disclosed high duty imports, Anti-Dumping/Countervailing duties (ADD/CVD), unallowable expenses, property tax values. Look for weaknesses on what they did not disclose that will end up in their pockets. There is justification for unreported value. The IRS net worth audit is an example of how to audit unreported value.

IRS Net Worth Audit

To catch the auditee, you must think outside the box like an IRS net worth audit. In the IRS net worth audit, the auditors take several years (usually 3 years) of beginning net worth with different categories of assets and liabilities and capital at beginning of year and compare this amount to the net worth at end of the year to calculate a delta. For cash basis taxpayers, bank statements are used to show the ins and out of transactions during the year. The net amount of cash transactions during the year is then compared to net income reported. Just because somebody reported a certain amount of net income does not mean that is all there is. There can be adjustments made for food, clothing, daily expenses, and gifts received in cash as an example. The only way out of this is cash in a mattress or safe. However, IRS Criminal Investigation Division can seize this as well. The power of the bank statement is difficult for auditees to overcome. It is difficult to explain increases in real estate, stock investments, automobiles, and other tangible assets when there is little to no net income reported on your 1040. There could be unreported net income as well! This fact is sometimes ignored in a lot of compliance audits and audits are primarily/entirely spent on reported/declared/proposed/incurred value.

There is a precedent for reviewing unreported value as mentioned earlier. To give an illustration, The IRS performs net worth audits which are usually part of Criminal Investigation Division, where they compare Net worth (Assets) of individuals or businesses at the beginning of the year compared to the end of the year and take that difference using bank accounts and compare to what was declared on tax return for net income that year with any appropriate adjustments, such as cash gifts by relatives.

This effectively will uncover unreported tax revenue not reported by the taxpayer.

Example would be:

	CY 2019	CY 2020	Difference
Cash	$10,000	$50,000	$40,000
Real Estate	150,000	300,000	150,000
Stocks	20,000	100,000	80,000
Autos	50,000	75,000	25,000
Total Assets	$230,000	$525,000	$295,000

Reported Tax Return

Income	$75,000	$100,000	$175,000
Subtract			
Food	6,000	6,000	12,000
Clothing	1,000	1,000	2,000
Gas	1,500	1,500	3,000
Utilities	1,500	1,500	3,000
Subtotal	$10,000	$10,000	$20,000
Total net Income	$65,000	$90,000	$155,000

In this case there is an unexplained difference of $140,000 ($290,000-$155,000). The question to the taxpayer would be how did your assets increase by such a large amount while your net income was not enough to fund the increase. I made this example simple as there are no liabilities or owner's equity. Any increase in either account would explain some of the asset increases. It would be difficult for the taxpayer to explain his/her way out of this predicament. The IRS could then put this into collections and go to civil or even criminal court to get the money.

IRS Criminal Investigation Division (CID) could also seize assets if judgment goes against the taxpayer.

US Customs Introduction to Unreported Value

My first introduction to unreported value occurred at US Customs Regulatory Audit. At that time, the Agency was doing Compliance Assessment audits using an audit program that had a lot of detailed audit steps. In the trade area of Value. 19 CFR 152.103 (a)(1) states that declared value shall be based on price paid or payable. One of the senior auditors there would mention auditing foreign vendor payments. This was not specifically in the audit program, so I asked him what he meant by that. He stated he was looking for "unreported value" which are hidden foreign wire transfer payments beyond what the company had declared to Customs. As I was a little familiar with IRS net worth audits, this concept made sense to me.

In addition, the Compliance Assessment audit program did actually include a detailed section called unreported value which included additions to price paid or payable. The audit program required sample testing using statistical sampling of imported merchandise that was declared to US Customs.

The compliance assessment audit program included the following steps for Unreported Value:

Indirect Payments - If a seller forgives a loan to the buyer instead of the buyer paying cash. Must be included in transaction value 152.103 (a)(2).

Supplemental Payments

Quota/Visa Payment – If paid for/by benefit of seller. Must be included in transaction value

Currency Exchange Adjustment

Other – (Possibly Foreign Vendor Payments analysis would be covered here).

Additions to price paid or payable

Selling Commissions 19 CFR 152.103(b(1)(ii)

Royalties – Included if a condition of sale in contract. 152.103 (f)

Assists – Tools, dies, molds provided at reduced cost or no cost to seller 19 CFR 152.103(d)

Proceeds – If seller receives additional payments after importation due to resale, etc. must be included in transaction value19 CFR 152.103(g).

Packing costs – Addition to price paid or payable, However, If third party performs packing for seller, seller may not include these costs in transaction value.152.103(b)(1)(i)

These costs would usually be reviewed by selecting accounts from G/L/Trial Balance by nomenclature or sampling.

Since the audit program allowed an auditor to review Other, this auditor would request total foreign vendor payments for the CY/FY from the importer auditee and compare to the total reported (declared value). If there was a large difference, he would zero in on specific vendors and review the vendor's transactions. He explained this was a good way to find additional payments, foreign assists/payment of liabilities provided by the buyer to the seller, etc. that were hidden by the importer by coding the transactions to innocuous accounts. I quickly starting utilizing his method. However, as time went by, Regulatory audit transitioned to Focused Assessment Testing which was based on auditor judgement instead of fixed audit steps and unreported value became completely forgotten, unless the auditor memorized the regulations or if a sample was randomly selected that pertained to unreported value.

The review of payments is grounded in the basis of appraisement which is transaction value or price paid or payable as shown:

Basis of appraisement Customs – Generally the basis of appraisement for value is transaction value or price paid or payable (19 CFR 152, Part C and E, 152,103). However, if the value is based on a related party transaction or can't be determined due to limitations etc.; Other valuation methods such as deductive value or computed value may be applicable. Therefore, you need to perform a review of payments, or price paid or payable. Tracing to checks or bank statements is the most reliable way to verify authenticity as made up or manipulated financial statements are always a possibility. Also, be aware of the payable part of the regulation which means look if the importer paid a liability off for the seller instead making a payment, that amount should be part of transaction value.

A good technique is to go back to source documents. Do not just rely on the general ledger/trial balance for small companies. Go back to the purchase order, invoice, bank statements/checks as less sophisticated accounting software can be manipulated or documents doctored. Remember to follow the money!

Many compliance audits will focus on reported value and ignore unreported value. Unreported value is what is not known through misclassification, hiding, obfuscation. See discussion below.

Methods to find Unreported costs on US Customs Audit

As stated above, this is under the Other Step in the Compliance audit program. (Possibly Foreign Vendor Payments analysis would be covered here) Take the total amount of foreign vendor payments for the CY/FY and compare to what was declared to US Customs. If there is a difference in the total amount, review by vendor to determine where the overpayments are. This is a step skipped by many auditors but I found it quite useful in identifying costs hidden by the company. I believe this method could be used on other compliance audits. For example, on a property tax audit, once an analysis is done identifying the vendors for the various property types reviewed (CIP, leases, Assets), an auditor can determine if all costs paid to the vendor for the year were reported in the property tax return which might disclose potential timing or miscoding to wrong accounts in the general ledger.

An example of foreign vendor payment analysis for US Customs would be:

Compare total declared value from ACS XX/XX/22:

Total declared value	$10,000,000

To total foreign vendor payments:

Total wire transfers to foreign vendors Or payments	$12,000,000

If there is a material difference between the total declared value and foreign payments to various vendors which in this case is $2,000,000 or 20% which is material, then you would look into the details of the foreign vendor payments by individual vendor or just select a statistical or judgmental sample of foreign vendor payments knowing that there is a substantial chance of unreported value out there in the universe of transaction payments. In addition, by randomly selecting foreign vendor payments and examining the invoices, shipping documents, and payments, this may also uncover problems with misclassification, ADD/CVD or other problems if these documents don't match the declared value on the government customs form.

I also review the General Ledger/Trial balance by nomenclature for potential assists for US Customs audits. Assists are "help" given by the buyer to the seller which should be declared to US Customs and results in undervaluation. On US Customs audits, I would review/sample accounts for tools, production costs, equipment to find assists as well.

DCAA Introduction to Unreported Value

Although not formally included in the audit program as unreported value, after determining what the contractor excluded as unallowable. I always reviewed General Ledger accounts by nomenclature for any additional unallowable/un-allocable/unreasonable costs risk (Unreported value) in DCAA audits not excluded by the contractor. Unallowable costs should be excluded from proposals/submissions and results in overcharging. On DCAA audits, I would review/sample accounts for potentially unallowable/un-allocable/unreasonable legal costs, marketing costs, technical literature/supplies, employee relation costs, and other accounts. I would also look for un-allocable costs by reviewing the composition of indirect pool and base costs as well reviewing direct costs for mischarging to the extent possible. I would also keep an eye out for unreasonable costs as well.

There is an audit performed by DCAA somewhat similar to unreported value, that attempts to determine if there was secret and/or updated information for FFP contracts that was not disclosed to the government at the time of proposal negotiations. Defective Pricing audits for DCAA look for current, accurate and complete information at the time of negotiations I do not favor these audits as they are post award audits of firm fixed price contracts. There are too many restrictions on these audits as the auditor has to establish that current, accurate, and complete information was not provided to the customer at the time of negotiations. Basically, the auditor would ask for purchase orders, labor estimates, budgets, that existed before the date of negotiations. This would expose secret/updated information known by the auditee that was not disclosed to the government. You can analyze over/underrun variances by cost element between estimates and actual costs incurred. This will give you leads on where the company might have hidden information on **underruns.** These audits are too restrictive versus incurred cost audits where an auditor can look at anything they want. It is difficult to uncover anything on these audits because the company can hide and not disclose information, they know they had available unless it just pops up randomly or an employee exposes the information.

I have experience in this area as I worked on DCAA's investigation team for six years. I assisted the US Attorney's Office in San Francisco on a Qui Tam case related to a secret IR&D budget that was not disclosed to the government. I calculated the questioned costs due to the defective pricing and helped in the negotiations. The government negotiated a $13 million settlement which was the largest settlement in Bay Area history at the time. Usually, as in this case, you need an inside person (employee) to rat on the company. The person who cooperated with the government received a portion of the settlement.

Section III
Risk Assessments for US Customs and DCAA Compliance Audits

US Customs Risk Assessment

In the Risk Assessment, you must take a martial attitude when performing this audit step. Put yourself in the shoes of the auditee. How can the auditee pay less Customs duties as an example? Basically, I want to understate the value and understate the duty rate so the company pays less tax. If I undervalue merchandise or deduct non-dutiable costs that works, if I misclassify items to a lower or $0 duty rate, that also works. If I falsify country of origin for FTA or claim a passthrough country (instead of actual country of origin) when I transship to avoid ADD/CVD that works as well. See tables below for a "brainstorming" matrix and how I would document this in a risk assessment for a US Customs Trade area. You must think like fraudster to catch the fraudster. You must attack before the adversary moves. You move first! We are not doing an investigation but an audit, but the thinking, planning, strategy does include a lot of aspects of what an auditor would do in a fraud investigation support role.

For US Customs, reported value is what is declared on a Customs tax form. This is what is known. Many compliance audits will focus on this and ignore unreported value.

Unreported value is what is not known through misclassification, hiding, obfuscation, assists, additional payments, etc. A final note, if you suspect fraud (Double set of books), the auditor can always trace back to the bank statements to ensure the payments shown in the trial balance/General Ledger are based in reality. At US Customs, some audits would compare the total foreign vendor payments by vendor totals to what was reported as imported value for US Customs. This would hypothetically disclose if there were extra payments, assists, or other transactions not reported to US Customs.
Risk is our business as an auditor. This is not supposed to represent every possible scenario of risk but the purpose of this is to get you

thinking of different scenarios that result in expanded profits by avoiding duties for the importer. Think about how you will exploit your adversary's weaknesses by attacking not where he is strong but where he is hiding something or misrepresenting costs that should be subject to duties and fees. It will be very difficult for him to squirm his way out of a situation where it looks like the company is taking advantage of the government by increasing profits by not paying duties for dutiable products by misclassification or undervaluing imports. Follow the money and that will usually lead you to where the problems are that you will have a high probability of prevailing. A radical alteration of thinking needs to occur. This is kind of like when the Beatles took LSD and expanded their minds and way of thinking!

Here is a matrix of the various risks encountered in a US Customs audit so that you can see the various manipulation schemes by the auditee by trade area, the reason for the manipulation scheme, and the documents the auditor would review to look for it:

US Customs Trade Area	Value	Classification, ADD	ADD	Unreported Value	ADD, FTA
Manipulation scheme by Company	Undervaluation	Misclassification	Transshipment	Assists/Additional Payments/ Unreported Value	Wrong COO
Why company does this	Lower value to lower duty/fees, ADD/CVD	Change classification to lower duty rate or non-dutiable or to avoid ADD	Put pass through country of origin to avoid ADD	Declare lower value, pay lower duty, extra payments not declared and no duty paid.	To get preferential treatment FTA, lower duty or non-dutiable or avoid ADD
Documents to review/Procedures	Invoice, CF 7501 for NDCs	Invoice	Bill of Lading Invoice	General Ledger/Trial Balance for assists	COO certificate for FTA
Documents to review/Procedures	Payments	Import Specialist review	Packing List Shipping Documents	Foreign Vendor Payments/ Payments summarized by Vendor for Unreported value	Bill of Materials for FTA, production records to meet % COO requirements
Documents to review/Procedures	Bank statements	Technical Specifications reviewed by import Specialist	Payment records, Bank Statements	Payment records, Bank Statements	Invoice Shipping Documents Bill of lading packing list, payments, bank statements

This matrix is to get you to think about how a This company can try to game and manipulate the system and the kinds of documents needed to catch them with the proverbial hand in the cookie jar.

The actual risk assessment will be more general. In a proper risk assessment, the auditor would identify: the risk trade areas, reasons for review and support for the decision, and areas not reviewed and the reasons why. Note I have included the concepts of reported (declared value and classification) and unreported (foreign vendor analysis, assists, misclassification, etc.) within the risk assessment.

An example of risk assessment would be

Trade Area	Regulation	Potential Problem	Document to Review	Reason for Selection
Value				
Declared Value	19 CFR 152.103(a)	undervalue	Invoices payments, bank statements	Required on Focused Assessment
Unreported Value	19 CFR 152.103(a)	Obfuscate total payments to a vendor	Foreign vendor analysis	To determine completeness of trade area
Assists, Additions to price paid or payable (Packing, etc)	19 CFR 152.103(b)(d)	Declare $0 by coding to other accounts in G/L	G/L/Trial Balance	To determine completeness of trade area
Classification	19 CFR 152.11	Misclassification to lower tariff rate or non-dutiable	Invoices, Technical Specifications	Required on Focused Assessment
ADD	19 CFR.351.211 19 CFR351.212	Misclassification to avoid ADD, undervaluation, transshipment	Invoices Shipping documents Payments, bank statements to check for undervaluation and verify COO	Potential for significant LOR and non-compliance
FTA	Harmonized Tariff Schedule (HTSUS) General Notes 3-35	Overvalue, or false claim for FTA, false Mfg. records to overstate Country of Origin (COO) production requirements for claim	Invoices Shipping documents COO documents, Mfg. Records, payment records, bank statements to verify COO	Potential for significant LOR and non-compliance

High Risk Areas in US Customs Audits

In a US Customs risk assessment, there are so many regulations, an auditor could spend a lifetime of study and still not know all the regulations and the potential trade areas that could be risk areas, such as: Value, classification, as well as Free trade agreements, ADD/CVD, Country of Origin, related party transactions, drawback, NDC deductions 19 CFR 152.102(f), etc.

Remember to follow the adversary and find the weak points – using risk assessment and audit program to find weak points to exploit, what could go wrong (WCGW, CPA), think of the risk assessment as the lifeblood of your audit. The risk assessment changes like a living thing.

Here are some high-risk areas to look out for in a US Customs Audit in order to do a proper risk assessment (Note: This list is not all inclusive):

Value - look for declared and unreported value,
Additions to price paid or payable
Selling Commissions 19 CFR 152(b)(1)(ii)
Royalties – Included if a condition of sale in contract. 19 CFR 152.103(b)(1)(iv)
Assists – Tools, dies, molds provided at reduced cost or no cost to seller 19 CFR 152.103(b)(d)
Proceeds – If seller receives additional payments after importation due to resale, etc. must be included in transaction value. 19 CFR 152.103(g)
Packing costs - If third party performs packing for seller, seller may not include these costs in transaction value. 19 CFR 152(b)(1)(i)

These additions to price paid or payable would usually be reviewed by selecting accounts from G/L/Trial Balance by nomenclature or sampling.

Antidumping – Check for undervaluation, wrong Country of origin (COO) by reviewing invoice, shipping documents, payments, bank statements to verify COO
High duty tariffs for areas such as textiles, etc. should warrant extra attention
FTA – Check for false Country of Origin (COO) certificates, manufacturing records to verify COO requirements, invoices, shipping records, payments, bank statements to verify COO
Non-Dutiable Cost deductions – unless actual freight costs, the costs should not be deducted from declared value. Verify to payments for freight costs, can't be based on estimates.
Disclosures by the company will give you leads on possible areas to review based on what caused the disclosed problems.
Related party, less than arms-length transactions – watch for undervaluation on purchase invoices from related parties 19 CFR 152.103(j)(2), lower declared value
Misclassification (lower duty rate or non-dutiable) which requires import specialist review
Undervaluation (lower declared value), by tracing to payments and bank statements
Transshipment (lower duty rate or avoid duty)
Additional payments (not added to value), Foreign vendor payment review
HTSUS Chapter 98 imports must meet certain requirements and is an area of risk
Drawback claims for 99% refund must meet certain requirement – verify claims meet various requirements 19 CFR 190, U.S.C. 1313

DCAA Risk Assessment

A DCAA risk assessment is quite complicated because it involves reported values in proposals, forward pricing rate agreements (FPRA), incurred cost audits for FFP and CPFF contracts. The DCAA risk assessment also includes unreported values related to contract costs included in proposals, FPRA, and incurred costs. Companies will try to include unallowable, un-allocable, and unreasonable costs that should not be included in proposals/submissions that are not known by the auditor because they are hidden by the defense contractor.

Since these areas are so broad, I have not included an example of a risk assessment like I did in the US Customs risk assessment above. I will instead present general concepts and information that will aid a DCAA auditor to create their own risk assessment based on the information in their audits. A DCAA auditor is responsible for determining if direct costs and indirect costs proposed/incurred on government contracts are allowable, allocable, and reasonable. A risk assessment for DCAA would focus on finding questioned costs due to unallowable, un-allocable, or unreasonable costs for proposals and incurred cost submissions. There are different cost impacts to the government depending on whether the government contracts are cost plus fixed fee (CPFF) or firm fixed price (FFP) contracts.

Verify that the direct and indirect costs are from the current period and the calculations for proposals/FPRA are accurate. The completeness (unreported) concept is a little bit different as it relates to proposals, FPRA, and incurred cost/ audits. The auditee submits unallowable and un-allocable costs. To determine completeness, review the General Ledger/Trial Balance by nomenclature for unallowable costs/risk for historical (prior) for proposals/FPRA and/or current CY/FY (incurred cost). Look for unusual account names like technical materials that might include advertising/public relations, or expenses like legal costs where costs may not be related to government contracts.

Reported Value in Proposals/Incurred Cost/Defective Pricing

In the reported value amount for DCAA, the auditee will try to include unallowable FAR 31.205 costs, un-allocable FAR 31.201-4 costs, and unreasonable costs FAR 31.201-3 in its submissions. In DCAA audits, there are two stages of audit, proposal and incurred cost/defective pricing. Initial proposal audits are based on forecasts. Companies will generally overstate proposed indirect rates and direct costs (direct labor, direct material, overhead, G&A) on FFP contracts in order to increase costs and profits to the government. For Cost reimbursable contracts, companies will also inflate the indirect rates and direct costs on proposals/estimates but will only benefit by increasing fees, only as the company will ultimately be paid on costs incurred.

The main goal in the proposal stage is to overstate direct costs and pool expenses and understate the allocation base in proposed indirect rates. Overstate proposed costs on CPFF contracts for additional fee, overstate proposed costs on FFP/FPRA to obtain excess costs and excess profits (defective pricing), mischarging to a different project, vague general ledger descriptions (technical publications could be advertising). Allocate Foreign and commercial costs to CPFF contracts. Shift from FFP to CPFF, Accounting and purchasing charged to overhead instead of G&A, for example.

Another example for training of mind purposes as it relates to over-estimating costs on firm fixed price (FFP) proposals is in the past, there used to be a dollar limitation on IR&D/B&P expenses which are reimbursable to the government through the G&A rate, so contractors with FFP contracts would always claim that they were going to increase IR&D/B&P expenses (at or below the dollar limitation) and decrease FFP R&D in proposals and FPRAs when historical indirect rates showed the opposite of this. (There was actually a decrease in IR&D/B&P) and increase in FFP R&D contract overruns.) The effect of the company proposing low amounts of FFP R&D direct labor and then overrunning the FFP R&D direct labor and underrunning both indirect costs and IR&D (to keep under the limit which was another incentive). This resulted in proposed Overhead and G&A rates being highly overstated on proposals when compared to historical rates for FFP contracts which turned into lower losses or higher profit for the company as the company was losing their shirts on FFP R&D contracts and egg foo young on the face for auditors who did not question this. As there is no longer a limit on IR&D/B&P, I do not believe this is occurring as much. If you run into this situation where there are majority FFP contracts. I recommend **questioning** the difference between proposed and historical rates as this is nothing but a contractor ploy as the company is probably overrunning on FFP contracts and need to do this to stay in business. Do not expect defective pricing audits to catch this as these are just bad "estimates".

In addition, when auditing direct labor estimates in Forward Pricing Rate Agreements (FPRAs) for FFP contracts, make sure the company takes into account probabilities of award in their inclusion of direct labor estimates. As I had one company that did not include these probable FFP R&D contract direct labor costs in the Overhead and G&A base even when there were greater than 50 percent probability of contract award. However, they would include 100% of IR&D labor costs regardless of probability and subsequently underrun the IR&D/B&P limitation and overrun the FFP R&D contracts again resulting in underrunning O/H and G&A rates.

Watch for this type of underrun on defective pricing audits. However, it is difficult to get "secret" budget and if auditor did not take exception at time of proposal/FPRA, probably difficult to prove anything there. Best to nip this at the bud at the proposal/FPRA stage if you ever see actual overhead and G&A rates underrunning proposed rates substantially because of this situation, my advice is question costs first ask for excuses by contractor later. Don't fall for this "cry wolf" strategy of how these future upcoming years forecasts is going to be different.

On cost reimbursable contracts, costs become incurred costs when the contract is completed. Companies will include unallowable costs charged to innocuous accounts, include commercial/foreign costs to allocate to government contracts and include unreasonable (interior design costs) when possible. The auditee will Include unallowable costs in the overhead and G&A pool. Unused/excess facilities costs are also unreasonable and should be questioned. Make sure Purchase discounts are deducted from direct material costs.

Defective pricing relates to FFP contracts at completion and company only has to show costs were current, accurate, and complete at time of negotiation. This is usually quite difficult unless you find an undisclosed forecast or purchase order. Follow the audit program and headquarters guidance. Do over/underrun analysis. For significant underruns which represents profits to the company, look deeper of why this occurred and whether it was possible the company knew something before the contract was negotiated.

I have included a matrix showing the effect of unallowable and unreasonable (indirect costs overhead (O/H) and G&A) costs on FFP and CPFF proposals, incurred costs, and defective pricing. Note that there can also be impacts due to direct costs (labor, material, subcontracts) questioned which are not included in this schedule. But the effects on the different type of contracts and audits are the same.

Unallowable, Unreasonable Costs Matrix

Proposal Stage	Type of Contract	Method of Auditing	Effect of not excluding Unallowable/Unreasonable Costs
Proposal/FPRA	CPFF	Review Proposed Historical G/L Trial Balance Accounts to verify exclusion	Fee
Proposal/FPRA	FFP	Review Proposed Historical G/L Trial Balance Accounts to verify exclusion	Cost plus profit, way more risk
Incurred Cost Stage	Type of Contract	Method of Auditing	Effect of not excluding Unallowable/Unreasonable Costs
Incurred Cost	CPFF	Review Historical G/L Trial Balance Accounts to verify exclusion	Cost plus potential penalties, high risk compared to proposal/FPRA stage
Post Award Audit	FFP	Defective Pricing, need non-disclosed budget with unallowable costs not excluded at time of negotiations	Cost plus penalties. Difficult to catch at this point. Much easier to catch at Proposal/FPRA stage.

To add context and additional details for the matrixes, I have summarized the risk for the different types of contracts included in the matrix above.

Company Risk for Cost Type Matrix Summary

Overstate proposed direct and indirect costs on CPFF contracts for additional fee. Watch for the inclusion of unallowable, unreasonable costs in O/H and G&A pools. Verify direct costs, Overhead, subcontracts, ODCs and unallowable O/H are included in the G&A Base. On Incurred cost audits, watch for allocation of costs from FFP/Commercial/Foreign contracts to CPFF contracts through including commercial/foreign costs and allocation manipulation between contract types to increase profits by avoiding overruns on FFP/Commercial/Foreign contracts. Contractor will be **paid** on CPFF type contracts due to shifting! The Contractor can usually get contract increases on CPFF contracts by asking the customer for additional funds, so even if CPFF contract is overrun, there is incentive to shift costs as they can get budget increases by asking for them with written justification. Look for unallowable, unreasonable costs in the O/H and G&A pools. Verify direct costs, Overhead, subcontracts, ODCs and unallowable O/H are included in the G&A Base

Company Risk for FFP Matrix Summary

Proposals/FPRA Overstate proposed costs to increase **costs** and profits, much greater risk than CPFF proposals which only increases fees. Verify that direct costs, Overhead, subcontracts, ODCs and unallowable O/H are included in the G&A Base. Also, the DCAA auditor must look out for proposals/estimates where the auditee overstates pool costs and understates the allocation base in proposed indirect rates. The company can also overstate proposed costs on FFP/FPRA to obtain excess profits (defective pricing), mischarging to a different project, vague general ledger descriptions (technical publications could be advertising) indirect pool, Related party transactions which sometimes overstate costs charged to the government.

Use analytical horizontal and vertical analysis to analyze proposed/incurred expenses from year to year to note any large variances for review.

Defective pricing audits – On these audits, the company will usually obfuscate or conceal current, accurate, and complete information available at time of proposal/FPRA negotiations when requested by auditors.

Detailed Explanation of Indirect Rate Calculations

In order to properly perform a proper risk assessment for DCAA audits, you must understand the calculation of indirect rates which include IR&D/B&P. The composition of indirect rates in DCAA is confusing and leads to a lot of manipulation by the company and errors due to lack of knowledge. I will provide more details on how indirect rates in DCAA are calculated to provide auditors with the tools they need to understand and audit these costs.
IR&D/B&P calculations are confusing. IR&D/B&P labor and direct costs should be accumulated separately from other direct and indirect costs.

IR&D / B&P Labor

IR&D / B&P Material

Overhead applied to IR&D / B&P labor

This calculation is achieved by including IR&D/B&P labor in calculation of Overhead rate as shown:

Overhead Rate:

Overhead Expenses

÷

Direct Labor + IR&D/B&P Labor

IR&D/B&P costs are then carried to the G&A pool and are excluded from the G&A base as shown:

IR&D/B&P Labor (IR&D/B&P)

IR&D/B&P Overhead applied

IR&D/B&P Material (IR&D/B&P)

Is then included in G&A pool expenses (and excluded from calculation in the G&A base). IR&D/B&P calculations are also shown in the calculation of indirect rates below to give you a complete picture.

Now I will explain the calculation of indirect rates to aid the auditor in the risk assessment and to catch mistakes in the calculations of indirect rates. Note the calculations include a fringe benefit rate which adds complexity.

Fringe Benefit Rate

Fringe Benefits pool – Payroll taxes, leave, etc. less unallowable costs

÷

Fringe Benefits allocation base - Direct Labor (Labor rate X Hours) + IR&D/B&P Labor (IR&D Labor rate X Hours) + Indirect Labor (Labor rate X Hours) (O/H and G&A)

=

Fringe Benefit Rate

Overhead Rate

Overhead Pool expenses – Production Support expenses (related to more than one contract) such as:

Indirect Labor, Fringes, Rent, training, etc. less unallowable costs

÷

Overhead Allocation Base - Direct Labor (Labor rate X Hours) + Fringes IR&D/B&P Labor (IR&D Labor rate X Hours) +Fringes

=

Overhead Rate

G&A Rate

G&A pool expenses - (CEO's salary, rent, training, etc.), fringes on G&A labor, IR&D labor, fringes, overhead on IR&D fringed labor, IR&D materials less unallowable costs

÷

G&A allocation base - Direct labor, fringe benefits on direct labor, overhead on fringed labor, direct materials, Other Direct costs, subcontracts, plus unallowable non-G&A costs.

=

G&A Rate

Audit of direct costs

Direct costs include:
Direct Labor (Direct labor hours x Direct Labor Rate)
Direct Materials (Direct Material unit price x quantity)
ODC such as travel
Subcontracts

Direct labor costs – I usually would verify the direct labor rates to payroll. Note that IR&D/B&P labor should be calculated and proposed separately from direct labor rates. Labor rates for IR&D/B&P are usually higher than direct labor rates. These rates should also be verified to payroll records.

For direct labor hours, I would request the technical engineer to review the hours from the Defense Contracting Agency.

I also performed a lot of floor-checks early in my career. I would review timecards and interview employees related to their charging on government contracts. You should review the timecards for any whiteouts, corrections, transfers from one contract to another contract which may indicate mischarging. Interviews with employees may also disclose information about charging. I believe these audits have merit and hope DCAA is still performing them.

For direct materials, other direct costs, review the backup support for the estimates. I usually obtain purchase orders, invoices, estimates from vendors, payments etc. Ensure purchase discounts are deducted.

For subcontracts, I would usually verify this to the proposal submitted from the subcontractor to the prime contractor to determine if everything matches. Sometimes the amounts for subcontracts are revised downward due to proposal negotiations which results in questioned costs.

Unreported Value Risk Assessment on Proposals, FPRA, Incurred Costs

Unallowable Costs in Proposals, FPRA, Incurred Cost audits

First determine what the company is excluding as unallowable costs. Then when you know that, turn your focus and look at costs that were not excluded. Study the adversary. Identify his strengths and weaknesses. Make sure you don't duplicate unallowable costs the company has already excluded. Focus on what they have **not** excluded and have included for payment by the government.

DCAA auditors are also responsible for auditing the allowability of direct and indirect costs charged to contracts. The DCAA auditor must perform an audit of indirect costs by reviewing the company's General ledger/trial balance to identify unallowable costs such as, technical materials (advertising) FAR 31.205-1, employee morale (entertainment) FAR 31.205-14, profit or loss on contract FAR 31.205-23, legal expenses (commercial patent) FAR 31.205-30.

For the proposal phase (pre-contract) of audit proposals and FPRA and the incurred cost phase of audits (when company finishes contract), for unallowable costs, scan general ledger/Trial balance by account nomenclature. Select accounts with suspicious (names or accounts that might be hiding unallowable costs such as technical materials, which sometimes includes advertising FAR 31.205-1. Employee morale can sometimes include unallowable alcohol/entertainment expenses FAR 31.205-14. Then review the high dollar amount details in each account selected. Select by vendor name and high value transaction amounts to identify unallowable costs hidden in general/ledger trial balance. Look for vendor names that might indicate advertising, large law firms which may include patent /commercial costs FAR 31.205-30.

Select accounts by nomenclature and high dollar amount for possible miscoding of unallowable expenses:

Technical supplies – Advertising FAR 31.205-1

Employee morale – alcohol, parties, entertainment FAR 31.205-14

Trade shows, meetings, conferences – Advertising FAR 31.205-1

Travel expenses – Massages, yes, I actually found expenses at contractor for employees getting massages in Japan, excess over per diem, air fare over coach without proper explanation FAR 31.205-46

Propose limousines instead of actual mileage using personal auto. A company with majority CPFF proposals with small amount of FFP proposals proposed limousine costs on every proposal to inflate the fees on CPFF contracts when employees actually drove cars and claimed mileage. FAR 31.205-46

Make sure that the company is including unallowable Overhead costs in G&A base. Some contractors don't include unallowable overhead costs in G&A. Watch out for this. FAR 31.201-6

If you have any questioned fringe/overhead (O/H) Rate, remember to apply questioned fringe/O/H rate to IR&D/B&P labor for additional questioned costs in the G&A pool.

If unallowable costs are identified in an account, consider performing vendor payment analysis on the vendors identified with unallowable costs to possibly identify additional (unreported) unallowable costs charged to the same or different accounts in the relevant time period audited.

Purchase discounts should be deducted from material costs. FAR 31.205-26

Watch for losses on other contracts claimed on incurred cost audits. As sometimes the company will try to claim this. FAR 31.205-23

Determine if residual values are deducted from fixed assets in calculation of allowable depreciation. This could result in lower depreciation expense in O/H and G&A pools. FAR 31.205-11

I like the direct approach to training for unallowable costs in relation to FAR 31.205. Why beat around the bush? If the real reason DCAA is here is to find non-compliances with FAR/CAS and protect the revenue, there should be an easier way to focus on what to look at in audits. I recommend training for auditors be made simpler by providing a quick list of unallowable costs and costs which are conditionally unallowable under certain conditions and allowable costs (low to no risk). That way auditors can start out knowing what to place their priorities on and think about the kinds of accounts they will test to find unallowable costs that might be miscoded or hidden.

The information should be right in front of new and experienced auditors so they can quickly access this information rather than having to go through the regulations in a piecemeal fashion and not seeing everything up front. Learning by slowly going through FAR 31.205 will take a long time and depending on memories to remember this information is risky as people tend to forget information as they get on in age.

The Training Officer can also recommend accounts/documents to review for the various accounts based on prior audit findings. For instance, I found expressly unallowable commercial patent costs in Legal expenses. I had to find the transaction in the General Ledger and review the invoice to determine that the costs were not related to the government under FAR 31.205-30. I have also found conditionally unallowable travel costs like Massages in Japan and first-class airfare which are not ordinary and necessary (reasonable) and therefore, unallowable by reviewing travel expenses in the general ledger and reviewing the invoices for travel samples

Expressly Unallowable costs to look out for in G/L/Trial Balance

FAR 31.201-5 – Credits 5 Purchase discounts should always be deducted from material costs claimed

FAR 31.205-1 -- Public Relations and Advertising Costs – Advertising costs unallowable, public relations allowable, Trade shows allowable only for foreign marketing

FAR 31.205-3 -- Bad Debts

FAR 31.205-7 -- Contingencies 72

FAR 31.205-8 -- Contributions or Donations

FAR 31.205-14 -- Entertainment Costs 92

FAR 31.205-15 -- Fines and Penalties, and Mischarging Costs 92

FAR 31.205-17 -- Idle Facilities and Idle Capacity Costs

FAR 31.205-20 -- Interest and Other Financial Costs

FAR 31.205-22 -- Lobbying and Political Activity Costs

FAR 31.205-23 -- Losses on Other Contracts

FAR 31.205-27 -- Organization Costs

FAR 31.205-30 -- Patent Costs – Unallowable unless required by contract

FAR 31.205-32 -- Precontract Costs – Unallowable unless approved by Government Official

FAR 31.205-49 – Goodwill 181

FAR 31.205-50 -- Executive lobbying Costs 182

FAR 31.205-51 -- Costs of Alcoholic Beverages 182

Conditionally Unallowable costs assuming certain conditions

FAR 31.205-2 -- Automatic Data Processing Equipment - Leasing Costs above market rate and related party

FAR 31.205-6 -- Compensation for Personal Services

FAR 31.205-11 – Depreciation – deduct residual costs, sales/leaseback, related party

FAR 31.205-33 -- Professional and Consultant Service Costs – reasonable and not based on recovery

FAR 31.205-35 -- Relocation Costs – some percentage restrictions on home sales/purchase

FAR 31.205-36 -- Rental Costs - reasonable, sales/leaseback limits

FAR 31.205-37 -- Royalties and Other Costs For Use Of Patents – allowable unless government has right to patent or not valid, related party

FAR 31.205-38 -- Selling Costs – reasonable and allocable, foreign selling unallowable

FAR 31.205-41 – Taxes – Federal taxes and some other taxes unallowable

FAR 31.205-42 -- Termination Costs -certain limitations apply

FAR 31.205-44 -- Training and Educational Costs – limited to post graduate and other limits

FAR 31.205-46 -- Travel Costs – Subject to FTR

FAR 31.205-47 – Costs Related to Legal and Other Proceedings unallowable if civil or criminal false claims proceeding with liability found on contractor

FAR 31.205-48 Deferred Research and Development Costs – unallowable precontract, allocable

FAR 31.205-52 -- Asset Valuations Resulting from Business Combinations Some limitations if purchased method used

Allowable Costs (low to no risk)

FAR 31.205-4 – Bonding Costs unless not required by contract, general allowable

FAR 31.205-5 -- Civil Defense Costs

FAR 31.205-10 -- Cost of Money

FAR 31.205-12 -- Economic Planning Costs

FAR 31.205-13 -- Employee Morale, Health, Welfare, Food Service, And Dormitory Costs and Credits

FAR 31.205-16 -- Gains and Losses on Disposition or Impairment Of Depreciable Property Or Other Capital Assets – included in contract costs

FAR 31.205-18 -- Independent Research and Development and Bid And Proposal Costs – Allowable but may be subject to advanced agreement

FAR 31.205-19 -- Insurance and Indemnification – allowable if reasonable

FAR 31.205-21 -- Labor Relations Costs 118

FAR 31.205-25 -- Manufacturing and Production Engineering Costs

FAR 31.205-26 -- Material Costs – adjust for credits

FAR 31.205-28 -- Other Business Expenses 130

FAR 31.205-29 -- Plant Protection Costs 130

FAR 31.205-31 -- Plant Reconversion Costs

FAR 31.205-34 -- Recruitment Costs – except for excessive compensation to pirate employees

FAR 31.205-39 -- Service and Warranty Costs

FAR 31.205-40 -- Special Tooling and Special Test Equipment Costs

FAR 31.205-43 -- Trade, business, Technical and Professional Activity Costs

FAR 31.205-45 -- Transportation Costs

Un-allocable Costs in Proposals, FPRA, Incurred Cost audits

In DCAA audits, Companies are required to perform accounting by contract (FAR 31.201-1). This brings up the concept of allocability (FAR 31.201-4). Direct costs are allocated directly to contracts while indirect costs are allocated through allocation bases to the contract. This raises the potential for mischarging, i.e., charging to a different contract versus the correct contract especially on FFP contracts as contract price is fixed while CPFF contracts are open ended to the contract price. Costs can also be misallocated through charging direct and/or indirect costs in the general ledger to contracts that should not receive the costs based on a causal/beneficial relationship.

Here is an example of contract mix allocation between commercial, foreign, government, FFP, CPFF, allocability – In this case the company has negotiated contracts of $23,000,000 and actual contract costs of $26,000,000 for total net loss of $3,000,000. Management decides to transfer (mischarge) costs from the FFP $1,000,000 and commercial contract $500,000 which are incurring large losses to the CPFF contract as shown:

	Contract A	Contract B	Contract C	Total
Contract Type	FFP	CPFF	Commercial	
Negotiated Amount	$10,000,000	$5,000,000	$8,000,000	$23,000,000
Actual Costs	12,000,000	4,000,000	10,000,000	26,000,000
Gain/(Loss)	(2,000,000)	1,000,000	(2,000,000)	(3,000,000)
Shift FFP costs <u>To</u> CPFF				
Through Transfer	1,000,000	(1,000,000)		
Adjusted Cost	11,000,000	5,000,000		
Gain/(Loss)	(1,000,000)	0		
Shift commercial Costs To CPFF				
Through Transfer		(500,000)	500,000	
Adjusted Costs		5,500,000	9,500,000	
After Transfer				

Total Costs after Transfer

	Contract A	Contract B	Contract C	Total
Contract Type	FFP	CPFF	Commercial	
Negotiated	$10,000,000	5,000,000	8,000,000	$23,000,000
Adjusted Cost	11,000,000	5,500,000	9,500,000	26,000,000
Gain/(Loss)	(1,000,000)	(500,000)	(1,500,000)	(3,000,000)
Net Effect	1,000,000	(1,500,000)	500,000	
Total				

Total Actuals vs Adjusted Costs

	Contract A	Contract B	Contract C	Total
Contract Type	FFP	CPFF	Commercial	
Negotiated	$10,000,000	5,000,000	8,000,000	$23,000,000
Actual Costs	12,000,000	4,000,000	10,000,000	
Adjusted Cost	11,000,000	5,500,000	9,500,000	26,000,000
Difference	1,000,000	(1,500,000)	$500,000	
Gain/(Loss)				($3,000,000)

Net effect of this is that company reduced their losses on FFP and commercial contracts by a total of $1.5 million and CPFF contract was increased by $1.5 million by transferring/mischarging costs between contracts. The total loss is still $3 million but is allocated differently with costs going to CPFF contracts which is now over the negotiated contract amount by $500,000 but with $1,000,000 now reimbursable by the US government. The Company can also ask for $500,000 additional funds for this overrun and get an increase in the contract price with some substantiation of the overrun by the company to the government. The overruns of FFP and Commercial contracts can't get overruns except due to equitable adjustment claim with Act of God/natural disasters necessary for recovery for FFP contracts, so the losses are not reimbursable. This is why there is a gold rush to shift costs to CPFF contracts on incurred costs. Misallocation of costs can be accomplished by transferring/mischarging direct or indirect costs from FFP, commercial contracts to CPFF contracts.

One of my most satisfying audit findings was related to allocability. I was auditing a company that we previously had no audit findings on incurred costs audits. I found that the company was including accounting and purchasing in the overhead rate. I knew that these costs are usually included in the G&A rate. I was wondering why the company was doing this.

Later, I discussed this issue with a technically competent Supervisory Auditor at DCAA, who explained to me the concept of allocability. Because there were more material and subcontract costs required for FFP contracts, more costs (for accounting and purchasing) were being allocated to cost reimbursable contracts versus fixed price contracts. The reason for this is the allocation base for overhead is based on labor while the allocation for the G&A base is total cost input which includes labor, materials and subcontracts. By including the accounting and purchasing costs in overhead, this resulted in allocating more of these costs to cost type contracts as these contracts are more labor intensive and have less materials and subcontract costs as they are usually more research related.

This is how an auditor increases their repertoire. I didn't really understand the implications, cause and effect, of allocability at the time, but after learning it, this problem was always in the back of my mind and I started looking for this same problem in all audits going forward. This resulted in a $65k impact on profits for this company in one year. I later found this problem at another contractor with a similar mix of business. This is similar to training in martial arts as you learn different sets and increase your knowledge gradually to become proficient. You must build up spiritually, physically, and mentally in order to succeed in martial arts.

Example of Risk Analysis Type of Contract – An auditor needs this type of analysis to see the whole contract mix and the possible manipulations that could take place. Besides unallowable, unreasonable, and commercial expenses being included in proposals/incurred costs, there is also a risk of shifting G&A to Overhead costs like purchasing and accounting so more of the costs will be absorbed by CPFF contracts as Overhead is allocated based on Direct Labor and FFP contracts here in this example include most of Direct Materials and subcontracts in the G&A base. The result of this shift would be a lower overhead rate and a higher G&A rate. You can see how more of the accounting and purchasing costs would be allocated to CPFF contracts based on direct labor if the same costs were included in overhead. More of the accounting and purchasing costs would go to FFP contracts and less costs would go to CPFF contracts, if the accounting and purchasing costs were included in the G&A pool. See example below where $50,000 in purchasing and accounting costs are reclassed from Overhead to G&A and the effect on CPFF and FFP contracts:

Allocation Example: Reclass of Accounting and Purchasing from O/H to G&A

	Contract A	Contract B	Contract C	
Contract Type	FFP	CPFF	Commercial	Total
Direct Costs				
Direct Labor	$500,000	$400,000	$300,000	$1,200,000
Direct Materials	$3,000,000	$50,000	$200,000	
ODCs	$50,000	0	0	
Subcontracts	$1,000,000	0	0	
Total direct costs	$4,550,000	$450,000	$500,000	$5,500,000
Indirect Costs				
Overhead Rate 50%	$250,000	$200,000	$150,000	$600,000
Total Cost Input	$4,800,000	$650,000	$650,000	$6,100,000
Including accounting and purchasing $50,000 G&A Rate (includes IR&D/B&P) 20%	$960,000	$130,000	$130,000	$1,220,000

Adjusted O/H Rate & G&A Rate

O/H Pool	$550,000 ($600,000 - $50,000)
O/H Base	$1,200,000
Adj. O/H Rate	45.83%
Adjusted G&A Rate	
G&A Pool	$1,270,000 ($1,220,000+$50,000)
G&A Base	$6,050,000 ($6,100,000-$50,000)
Adj. G&A rate	20.99%

Effect of reclass of Purchasing and Accounting
From O/H to G&A

	Contract A	Contract B	Contract C	
Contract Type	FFP	CPFF	Commercial	Total
Direct Labor	$500,000	$400,000	$300,000	$1,200,000
Overhead Rate 50%	250,000	200,000	150,000	
Overhead Rate 45.83%	229.150	183.320	137,490	
Reclass purchasing/accounting				
Difference Decrease	20,850	16,680	12,510	

Due to O/H Reclass

Total Cost Input	$4,800,000	$650,000	$650,000	6,100,000
Total Audit Adj. Costs	$4,779,166	$633,334	$637,500	$6,050,000
Proposed G&A Costs 20%	$960,000	130,000	130,000	
Audit Adj. G&A Costs 20.99%	1,003,230	132,948	133,822	
Difference (Increase)	($43,230)	($2,948)	($3,822)	
Due to G&A purchasing/accounting reclass				
Net effect on contract	($22,380)	$13,732	$8,688	

Check DCAA Formula

Questioned O/H Rate	4.17%
X Proposed Base	$400,000
Questioned Costs	$16,680

Questioned Base	$16,680
X Audit Adjusted G&A Rate	20.99%
Questioned Costs	$3,501

Questioned G&A Rate (Increase)	(0.99%)
X Proposed Base	$650,000
Questioned Costs	($6,435)

Total Questioned Costs $16,680 + $3,501- ($6,435) = $13,746 (Rounding Difference between $13,732)

The net result of this reclass to the federal government is a decrease to CFPP contract of $13,732 which is like a refund to the government and an increase to FFP contract of ($22,380), which is not reimbursable. Note: I did not calculate effect of the Overhead rate adjustment due to IR&D/B&P labor in the G&A pool as that is beyond the scope of this book.

As a reminder, firm fixed price foreign and commercial contracts are considered fixed negotiated price which includes costs plus profit. Cost overruns are not reimbursable.

CPFF, cost reimbursable contracts are based on actual costs incurred plus fee. These contracts are subject to modifications/increases. Cost overruns are reimbursable with substantiation.

Other examples of Un-allocable costs

Legal expenses - Patent costs not allocable to government, usually commercial FAR 31.205-30

Purchasing and accounting charged to overhead instead of G&A FAR 31.201-4 when there is a mix of FFP and CPFF contracts.

Any accounts in T/B G/L if you determine there are commercial and/or foreign costs commingled with government.

Unreasonableness of costs in Proposals, FPRA, Incurred Cost audits

DCAA auditors are also responsible for auditing costs for reasonableness FAR 31.201-3. Costs charged to government contracts must be ordinary, necessary expenses. What is a good barometer of reasonableness, ordinary and necessary? Comparison to market rate/value is a good position to take. The auditee will have a harder time trying to prove the costa are ordinary and necessary if the costs are a lot more expensive than what the market is selling for.

In line with this thinking, watch for personal non-business expenses, unnecessary expenses such as interior design commission costs by owner's wife (compare to cost of hiring a purchasing person), Related party (need to compare rent charged by owner to market rent), unused excess facilities.

Costs are reasonable if they are ordinary and necessary. Reasonableness (comparison to market) FAR 31.201-3. This is how a DCAA auditor would question costs for the famous $600 toilet!

Examples of unreasonable costs
Personal expenses for employees or family

Interior design greater than purchasing department costs

Accounting system developed internally versus purchasing one on market

Related party rent, auto expense, etc. where amount charged greater than market

Employee settlement costs where company most likely would most likely lose or lost, if case went to court are unreasonable and unallowable. (DCAA HQ Guidance)

Massage cost for employees included in travel expense

Limousine costs in excess of actual mileage cost of personal automobiles

Other General tips on DCAA risk assessment

My recommendation is to occasionally go back to source documents, time sheets, payroll, purchase requisitions, purchase orders, subcontracts, accounts payable, and review to see if there is anything funny going on such as changing contract numbers using whiteout, corrections, transfers between contracts problems.

Review indirect rate structures to determine if the correct allocation base is being used for the allocation pool based on a causal/beneficial relationship per FAR 31.201-4. For example, consider recommending material overhead rate if there are significant amounts of direct materials and large subcontracts. This could shift more costs to FFP and non-government contracts as these types of contracts generally use more of these costs than CPFF contracts.

If you make audit adjustments to estimated direct or indirect costs (not unallowable costs) on a Forward Pricing Rate Agreement (FPRA), ensure that you adjust the relevant allocation bases and/or IR&D/B&P and re-calculate the indirect rates to account for the audit adjustments for each FY/CY. I recommend using the contractor's FPRA electronic spreadsheet to calculate your audit adjustments, if possible.

Also, review contract labor by temporary agencies and see where the labor charges go to direct, indirect, or administrative and see if those categories match the invoices, pay rates, etc. There could be allocation issues here if the costs are charged to G&A pool expenses when they should have been charged to overrun FFP/commercial contract(s). The adjustment would be to reduce the G&A pool for the contract labor and increase the G&A base by the same amount as other direct cost. This would have the effect of reducing the G&A rate resulting in overall cost savings to the government as some costs would be allocated to overrun FFP and non-government contracts.

Don't forget to include a Schedule of direct and indirect costs on incurred costs audits. Use audit adjusted direct and indirect costs in the schedule.

Utilize horizontal/vertical analysis methods or artificial intelligence to identify large variances in direct and indirect costs that you may want to review in proposals, FPRA, and incurred cost audits. Determine what caused the increases and if the basis for the increases were valid if they are estimates. If actuals, identify the transactions and sample review based on nomenclature or anything suspicious that doesn't make sense.

Section IV
Recommendations to perform vendor payment analysis on Property Tax Audits and other procedures

As I have never performed any compliance audit work on property tax audits, this represent my own personal thoughts on what I would recommend/include in a property tax risk assessment. These are just the opinions/recommendations of a retired compliance auditor who is currently not employed in the auditing field who has extensive compliance audit experience at two federal agencies. I am basing my opinions/recommendations primarily on my experience at US Customs Regulatory Audit, which is somewhat similar to property tax audits in that in both audits, auditees try to reduce the tax base. Please take whatever I say with a grain of salt. If you incorporate any of these ideas in your audit, be sure to get your management to approve any steps you take from me.

Review dates on source documents, etc., to determine they are from the correct CY/FY. Accuracy can also be checked pretty easily by verifying the math and tax rates to accounting records and agency tax tables. However, how do you know the property tax statement values are complete? This is where the concept of reported and unreported value come in.

Reported Value for Property Tax Audits

First determine what the company is reporting in asset categories/classifications. Then when you know that, look at costs that may not have been declared correctly. Study the adversary. Identify his strengths and weaknesses.

For tax compliance audits look at components of how taxes are calculated, tax rate multiplied by taxable value usually and determine ways companies/owners can get around paying. The ways to get around paying tax is to lower values to $0 if possible, or lower tax rates for a different category/classification and not include all value (installation costs, unreported leasing, CIP, etc.) or make deductions from value that are not valid (tax exemptions). Company can also shift costs to wrong year in an accrual or cash accounting system. Other methods include undervaluation of assets by separating into smaller invoices (to avoid capitalization), miscoding assets to expense or other G/L non-asset accounts instead of capitalization of assets, timing differences, Related party transactions where assets are undervalued.

Also, in the review of different categories/classification of assets on the property tax statement: CIP, computer, real property, equipment, property belonging to others, government property, leased or rented property, supplies, other assessable assets, I recommend utilizing the California State Board of Equalization ASSESSORS' HANDBOOK SECTION 506. This document was created by the California State Board of Equalization and I have never utilized it in my role as an auditor.

There is a great checklist for various assets subject to property tax with information is California Board of Equalization ASSESSORS' HANDBOOK SECTION 506 PROPERTY TAX AUDITS AND AUDIT PROGRAM MARCH 2015, APPENDIX E, SAMPLE AUDIT CHECKLIST (Note: This checklist is available to the public on the internet,https://boe.ca.gov/proptaxes/pdf/ah506.pdf).

I have included a copy of a portion of the sample audit checklist related to leases. If the property tax auditor found any leads from asking these questions. The auditor should revise the audit program to include leases. He would then revise the risk assessment to include the sample audit checklist as the basis for including leases as an area of risk. There would then be a workpaper section on leases with a summary of any non-compliances and loss of revenue associated with leases on samples selected. There would also be leases in the audit report if there are exceptions noted. As I point out in my Chapter on Organizing, there is a connectedness between all stages of the audit and you must be flexible and react to any changes and information that occur during the audit. This is a terrific way to verify reported costs for property tax audits.

4. EQUIPMENT OUT ON LEASE OR RENT TO OTHERS
A. Does this company lease or rent equipment to others? Yes No
If yes: Type of Equipment:
Standard lease/rental period:
Reported at proper trade level? Yes No
Costs include: Sales Tax Freight Installation
B. Is the leased equipment reported to applicable California counties? Yes No
C. Does this company lease equipment to "related" entities at a lower value than those unrelated? Yes No
D. Does this company lease equipment originally purchased from a parent or subsidiary company in which they receive a discounted price? Yes No
E. Were lease contract agreements reviewed? Yes No
Comments/Notes:

Unreported Value for Property Tax Audits

Based on my concept of completeness, I would recommend that on property tax audits, auditors also perform an analysis by vendor to determine if there are any additional property value subject to tax that was not disclosed in the property tax return due to timing differences, potential miscoding to wrong account in general ledger, and or fraud. Vendors involved in asset purchases, CIP transactions, leases, improvements, computers, and inventory could be included in analysis for vendors with material balances.

Basically, all material taxable asset categories/classifications subject to a tax rate in the property tax statement could be included in this analysis. The auditor could select the asset categories to review based on risk assessment and then compare the difference between beginning and ending balance of payments to the various vendors involved with fixed assets to the net amount shown in the property tax statement. The auditor could then select asset categories/classifications with significant differences and take some judgmental samples of larger amounts to determine if all transactions were included.

This step was performed at US Customs Regulatory Audit but as time went on, less and less auditors performed this step as unreported value was included in the audit program in earlier years but was removed and replaced with an audit program based more on auditor judgment.

Therefore, for property tax auditors, you could perform this step if the interviews, questionnaires, and checklists do not give you enough information about all asset categories that you choose to review. The compliance auditor's business is Judgment and Risk. Don't be afraid to use your individual judgment and take calculated risks to find non-compliances and loss of revenue as long as you are following audit program, risk assessments, and rest of required audit steps with management approval and you are performing a professional, objective, factual audit informing the company of everything you are doing throughout the audit. This is the essence of this book and what I am trying to get across.

Example of vendor analysis for Construction in Progress (CIP)

Construction in Progress	XX/XX/2022
Property Tax Statement	$21,000,000
General Ledger/Trial Balance	$21,000,000
(Net increase/decrease)	
GL/TB breaks down by vendor	
XXX Construction Co.	$7,000,000
YYY Construction Co.	$10,000,000
ZZZ Construction Co.	$4,000,000

Payments Net for Year

XXX Construction Co.	$7,000,000
YYY Construction Co.	$12,000,000
ZZZ Construction Co.	$4,200,000

Under this example, I believe there is high risk of additional revenue in Vendor Construction Co. YYY construction as there is a big discrepancy between payments and G/L Trial Balance. The next step would be to question Construction Co. YYY about the differences and select samples to try to identify the differences. I would also review the payments to the vendor ZZZ Construction Co. matching general ledger amounts to payments and anything that doesn't match, I would question further. However, the difference is not very material, so the audit work I would perform would be commensurate with the risk.

Besides the three different audits I have described, I believe the more general parts of this book can be used on most if not all compliance audits. Taking or having a martial attitude towards auditing could be used on all types of audits. Uproot the adversary (an ounce of energy can defeat 1000 pounds) - By knowing adversary, ask right questions, select right accounts, get right evidence, evaluate sample to objective.

Section V
Materiality

I will now bring up the concept of Materiality in planning and risk assessment. For planning purposes select the largest amount transactions and/or balances. For risk assessment purposes, the order of preference to focus your resources on is:

Non-compliances with significant LOR

Non-compliances with low/little LOR

Non-compliances with no LOR

For LOR materiality, I focus on LOR first and Non-compliance second. I would spend the most time and effort on potential non-compliances when they are both material in amount and result in significant LOR. However, any non-compliances you find must be noted for follow-up and cleaning up internal controls/systems. My focus on LOR is related to follow the money which is the main purpose in my opinion. A non-compliance with little or no money is not nearly as important as a non-compliance with significant amounts of LOR (money). Which situation would the company want the auditor to pursue? That gives you the answer. These people want to get paid! So, the answer is the pocketbook!

Is there a dollar amount for you to review? This is not like financial accounting where there is a dollar threshold for materiality and whether to write errors off. Of course, the compliance auditor should focus on high dollar transactions and accounts to select samples. However, if non-compliances are found with loss of revenue, even if the loss of revenue is small, it should be reported and the company should quantify loss of revenue. Non-compliances with no or negative LOR should be reported as it may result in errors and/or positive loss of revenue in the future. The main purpose is to get company to comply and collect loss of revenue, if any.

Section VI
Fraud Assessment

In addition, you must perform a fraud assessment in accordance with GAGAS. When reviewing for fraud, always follow the money and think of ways the auditee can benefit, if they do not comply with regulations. Be objective in your review and do not let personal feelings you may have about a mom-and-pop shop type business to get in the way of fraud analysis. Always base your audit opinions on objective facts. Use prior audits, company disclosures, any problems noted by government customers, etc. If there are enough problems noted, consider a referral to Investigations. Your workpaper should state the probability of fraud occurring based on evidence.

Section VII
Cite the Specific Government Regulation

Also, always denote the relevant government regulations in your workpapers. This will solidify your risk assessment. Because if you can't name the government regulation that is non-compliance you may not have a finding! This also makes it easier when you summarize any non-compliances and LOR. You must first research and understand the government regulations of your particular agency. Then determine if the auditee is complying with the regulations through testing of samples. This will ultimately make it easier when you are writing your audit report as the non-compliances will be better supported with the government regulations properly documented and easily traced back to the workpapers and support.

The government regulations are usually spelled out in the audit program and in the government regulations you are working with. This is a very important step that I learned during my time on the Quality Assurance team at US Customs RA.

When I started on that team, we had a QA checklist that we used to determine the agency's compliance with GAGAS standards. However, the Supervisor at the time noticed that the checklist did not list the actual standard that was not being followed. This led to a lot of deficiencies being written up without a proper basis. She revised the QA checklist to include the specific references and voila! It became more difficult to find and document any deficiencies as they had to directly relate to a specific standard. I found this most enlightening.

I recommend to the extent possible to cite the specific regulation in non-compliance so that you have a much better chance of sustaining your findings. It will also reduce the number of deficiencies you will come up with naturally, because if you can't cite a government regulation, your finding may not be solid or something even reportable. Any finding that results in a non-compliance and LOR must include the specific government regulation. If you can't cite the specific regulation, you must drop the issue as it will result in losing and loss of credibility.

Sometimes you may have a recommendation for improvement or something that may improve something at the auditee, but if you can't cite a regulation, there is no non-compliance or LOR. In terms of your audit, Government regulations should be in the Source part of workpapers at a minimum and the in the other parts of your workpapers if you are citing a non-compliance or finding. Government regulations are also usually stated in the audit program. You should also include government regulations in your audit report for findings/non-compliance in the Criteria section and other relevant parts of the audit report.

Section VIII
Some other things to consider on your risk assessment

Communicate with the auditee (adversary) throughout your audit and keep a professional relationship. Actually, at the risk assessment stage of the audit, you can communicate the areas of concern to the auditee and your reasoning because you will soon request samples from those areas soon enough!

If you follow these steps, I believe you will eventually develop your own style of compliance auditing similar to Bruce Lee's Jeet Kune Do, which incorporates various martial arts together. Maybe someone will eventually write a follow-up to this book improving on what I have written.

This is not an all-inclusive list of what an auditor should do in a risk assessment. I am presenting this so that you THINK like a martial artist. Find the adversary's weakness and attack parts of the body versus the whole body. You must be flexible and move. Static defense will result in loss. Think like your adversary. How can I take advantage of the government and increase my cash flow and that will usually lead you to the promised land.

In risk assessment and audit program determine where adversary auditee can benefit from doing something that will result in a benefit to them and disadvantage to government. Don't just look at what the company declared/submitted, also look for unreported value transactions.

Martial arts approach to risk assessment

Control adversary

In order to control your adversary, you must approach him in a position of strength. How do you do that. Technically you must be strong. Your objective solid. Your planning complete and risk assessment well thought out.

Your results must also be solid. ensure your calculations of LOR are correct, cite correct regulations of any errors. Your workpapers and audit report must be solidly supported.

The risk assessment is the most important workpaper a compliance auditor prepares because this is where you will plan to get the most LOR and non-compliances while using the limited information and resources available to the compliance auditor. The cat and mouse game with the company begins here. As my first boss told me on my only interview with DCAA, this is where a GS-7 can face down a CFO and other finance officers of a company and beat them out. I think what he was talking about was the risk assessment when he told me that and it is indeed possible. You just have to know how and have the right martial attitude to do it!

The genius of Bruce Lee as a martial artist was because he would not use a fixed style but blended different martial arts together to create Jeet Kune do. He used what worked and rejected what didn't and fighting was the true test of one's skills. Auditing is similar in that instead of one way of thinking, you must be open to new ideas (like mine) in addition to the training and experience you get at your government agency and finding LOR and non-compliances in your audit are the crucible, if you can unearth them!

I would recommend that Training Officers for government agencies should summarize What Could Go Wrong (WCGW) in a quick list for all risk areas and distribute this to new auditors to get them thinking like this right at the beginning of their careers. Keep it all in one place and the auditors can reference the risks for whatever comes up in future audits in areas which results in non-compliances and significant loss of revenue. Training offices can look at prior audits and based on non-compliances and loss of revenue on audits that were successful, summarize all that can go wrong as well as what documents, interviews, etc. were used to succeed in getting the audit results pushed through and/or use my /way of marital thinking/methodology of risk assessment. Put it all in one place, instead of spread out over a manual or book to make it easy for the auditors to think like the company on how it is going to get away with their obfuscations for areas known to have risk. There should be an annual training course with Gung Fu auditing methodology! I believe establishing this martial attitude at the beginning of a compliance auditor's career is necessary as over time the auditors may get disillusioned and jaded if they keep performing audits with no findings.

I believe this quick list set of risks could possibly be carried over to financial auditing. The real risk on financial audits is material misstatement in the financial statements with emphasis on overstating net income/and or assets or understating liabilities/expenses. Financial auditor trainers can go through prior findings and identify areas where findings were found and reported. A quick list could be created and used in conjunction with traditional training methods. This would also satisfy fraud training requirements for compliance auditors. A concentration and focus on these proven problem areas could prove useful to new auditors right at the beginning of their careers so when a certain transaction or area comes up in their audit, the auditor can refer to the quick list and get a better idea of what the company may be trying to get away with and what kind of transactions to identify. The auditor can then determine if any kind of manipulation is occurring which could or has led to a material misstatement. More sophisticated schemes could also be included with newer ones.

An example of a quick list for US Customs

Trade Area	Value	Potential Problem	Document to Review
Value			
Declared Value	19 CFR 152.103	undervalue	Invoices payments, bank statements
Unreported Value	Regulation	Undervalue total payments to a vendor	Foreign vendor analysis
Assists, Additions to price paid or payable (Packing, etc)	19 CFR 152.103(b)(d)	Declare $0 by coding to other accounts in G/L	G/L/Trial Balance
Classification	19 CFR 152.11	Misclassification to lower tariff rate	Invoices, Technical Specifications
ADD	19 CFR.351.211 19 CFR351.212	Misclassification to avoid ADD, undervaluation, transshipment	Invoices Shipping documents Payments, bank statements
FTA	HTSUS General Notes 3-35	Overvalue, or false claim for FTA, false Mfg. records to overstate claim	Invoices Shipping documents COO documents, Mfg. Records, payment records, bank statements

Notice this is a copy of the risk assessment with reason for selection removed. This is another example of connectedness and how the audit is connected together. The audit agency trainers can take information from the risk assessments on completed audits with findings, which were agreed to by the company, and create quick lists of potential areas to review.

Chapter 2C
Reverse Auditing

This is a term and audit methodology that I created. What if your audit agency (DCAA) s auditing one of the largest defense contractors with a suboffice of 30 to 40 auditors on-site? The Suboffice has been there since the 1970s. Throughout the years on proposal audits and incurred cost audits, very little if any questioned costs were found and the company was determined to be relatively low risk due to the lack of audit findings. In the most recent Incurred Cost audit for 199X, the only questioned costs were some relatively immaterial Overhead costs and employee settlement costs for harassment of employees (sexual and discriminatory). The auditee did not agree with the employee settlement costs. The Overhead head costs were relatively immaterial. The company was a multi-billion-dollar contractor with a very high percentage of CPFF contracts. Suppose the risk assessment did not identify any risk areas other than what was found over the years, what would you look at?

I was given the assignment of reviewing G&A expenses for CY 199X. Without any audit leads or knowing the contract mix other than a very high percentage of CPFF contracts, I was supposed to evaluate the allowability, allocability, and reasonableness of General and Administrative expenses (G&A). I had no idea what to do. How would I do a complete audit and attempt to find questioned costs when so many auditors before in the decades previously had failed to find anything significant. How could I get a complete picture of what was going on and feel comfortable that I knew my adversary and could attack his weak points.

I started out by asking the contractor for a breakout of G&A expenses by account by month electronically, but was told by the company that this was not available. Therefore, I decided to take things into my own hands. I asked the company where their General Ledger/Trial Balance

(G/L) was. The CY 199X GL was located in the middle of the accounting department in 12 separate monthly hanging binders with computer printout pages approximately the size of 24 inches by 24 inches, each weighing about 20-30 pounds. It seemed like a daunting task to go through all this information, but once I was able to identify which part of the G/L reports were related to G&A, it went a lot easier! I would review all the transactions incurred in all 12 months by account by flipping through the pages. I would identify specific transactions I wanted to look at using the following criteria:

Account Name	Account No.	Vendor Name	Account Description	Regulation	Amount
Technical Supplies	XX-XXXX	Air Magazine	Advertisement for magazine	FAR 31.205.1	$100,000
Legal Expense	XX-XXXX	XXX & Sons Law Firm LLC	Legal Expenses	FAR 31.205-33	$1,000,000
Trade shows	XX-XXXX	Phoenix Exhibit Hall	Trade Show Fees	FAR 31.205-1	$200,000

I reviewed the vendor names and account descriptions to determine if there was anything suspicious and also concentrated on large amounts so I wouldn't waste my time on small amounts. I then matched the vendor names and account descriptions to the account name and account no. so that I could make a complete list of transactions I could request information from the auditee. Notice that the account names and descriptions include selections that are potentially unallowable, unreasonable, or un-allocable.

After several days of going through and writing all this information down from the G/L, I had put together a sample plan! I then put together a list of transactions I selected for samples to review and gave them to my contractor representative. After a few weeks, the company provided me with the backup support documentation for the sample I had selected. Much to my surprise, the advertisement charged to technical supplies account turned out to be an ad in a magazine. The ad showed a cell phone that used a satellite so that the person making it could call from the jungle or any place in the world. This seemed like real cutting-edge technology. So, I consulted with our government technical specialist engineer onsite at the contractor. He informed me that the government did not use these types of phones and the phones were definitely for commercial use. This was a new development! DCAA was completely unaware that this defense contractor was involved with any commercial products or business. The risk of the company getting subsidized by charging the government for commercial costs just went through the roof. I predicted at this point, that I would find more.

Like clockwork, when reviewing trade shows and marketing, it was unclear as to whether these costs were related to government or commercial work and on a legal expense, the company would not give me the backup support until after repeated requests. Finally, I sent them a list of requests to clear up these issues. Their response was that the legal expenses were related to non-government patent expenses which they agreed was unallowable. They also agreed the advertising was unallowable as well as 50% of the trade shows and marketing. This is a pretty good haul, considering decades of audits had not disclosed anything at this company.

I was also able to resolve employee settlement expenses based on DCAA Headquarters Guidance. The guidance stated that if the company was going to prevail in the legal case, the costs were unallowable. I went through the employee settlement legal files and based on the legal conclusions by the company's attorney, questioned significant costs. The company stated I was a little prejudiced on my analysis but did not disagree with me, opening up the possibility of negotiations.

My supervisor, Branch Manager, and everyone at DCAA did not understand how I had found these costs. I expected a pat on the back or some recognition but received none. To this day, I don't believe anyone at DCAA understands the methodology I used as it is so out of the box. The importance of knowing your adversary stands out here.

That's how the contractor was able to get away with clean audit reports for all these years. I would not recommend anyone follow this methodology unless perhaps as a last resort. If the risk at the company being audited is always low and/or non-existent and the auditors do not know the adversary, reverse auditing may be justified. The audit team would not have to review all 12 months of data like I did. They could just look at a one or two months of transactions with the highest expenses for the year. Selectively reviewing transactions using my method could be useful to really understand what is going on at a company. Since the company had a very high percentage of CPFF contracts, the millions of dollars I questioned were almost all reimbursed to the government.

This is the first and probably only time this contractor agreed to DCAA findings up to this point in time, as I am the only person who knew about using this methodology. I did not document this in my workpapers because, this would have required taking copies of the heavy binders and my supervisor did not care about how I selected my sample since there was very little to no risk based on prior decades of audits. In addition, her job before DCAA was repossessing cars in Hawaii and her hobby while at work was playing crossword puzzles. Just randomly selecting a few transactions is not going to cut it if you don't understand what is going on at the company and the true risk (commercial) which was hidden very carefully by the contractor. The auditor must be able to outthink his adversary but he/she must have the knowledge and information to do so on an objective, professional, and intellectual level. Sometimes you have to take the offensive, think outside of the box. In a situation with nothing to lose, why not take a chance and try my Reverse Auditing method. If nothing else you will prove to yourselves that the company is not concealing or obfuscating something.

If complying with GAGAS is a concern in relation to planning, Management can also consider doing a probe (1 month or 2 months of data) of reverse auditing and if any leads come up, the auditor can revise the audit program and risk assessment. Basically, use this as a "reverse" planning step or a more detailed walkthrough. The truth is if the risk assessment is very general and not detailed due to lack of audit leads/prior findings at the company, as was the case in my audit, reverse auditing could be used and justified as judgmentally selecting a sample. This is a balls to the walls approach if nothing else is working which can be justified given the right circumstances.

After this audit, I left DCAA soon after, as I realized I was never going to get recognition at DCAA, but I improved my audit skills which prepared me as I went on to US Customs. At my going away luncheon at DCAA after 13 years there, my Branch Manager, finally gave a speech and did mention my accomplishments and he said he was surprised at my growth as an auditor as he was also my first supervisor at DCAA. I appreciated that, but it was not enough, as I wanted a promotion and recognition.

Funny, but the only recognition I got was actually from the auditee. My contact invited me to get a free hot dog lunch at a party the company was hosting after the company had agreed to my findings. I was actually quite surprised by this, as our contacts at this defense contractor usually treated us like a colony of lepers. While eating the hot dog, I felt a warm feeling inside. So, this is victory! This feeling was so fleeting. The company's recognition meant more to me than any recognition I would've received from DCAA, if they had given me any. Because that is the true test. The crucible is winning a fight. The adversary acknowledges this.

After I left DCAA after 13 years, I eventually got some recognition at US Customs but no promotion in my 18 years there. To this day, I feel like I was robbed at DCAA. I felt that I had attacked a big, powerful adversary (defense contractor) which had unlimited resource, that I did not know anything about his fighting style in advance in a fight and based on my instincts and fighting skills knocked him out and defeated him. I always wonder why this was not recognized as a serious accomplishment at DCAA.

Again, this is not supposed to represent every possible scenario of risk but the purpose of this is to get you thinking of different scenarios that result in expanded profits for the contractor or less of a loss on fixed price contracts. Think about how you will exploit your adversary's weaknesses by attacking not where he is strong but where he is hiding something or misrepresenting costs that should be unallowable or unallocable. It will be very difficult for him to squirm his way out of a situation where it looks like the company is taking advantage of the government by increasing profits or lessening losses on fixed price contracts by mischarging. Follow the money and that will usually lead you to where the problems are that you will have a high probability of prevailing. A radical alteration of thinking needs to occur. This is kind of like when the Beatles took LSD and expanded their minds and way of thinking!

Chapter 2D
Internal Control Review

I am going to limit my discussion on review of internal controls. This is a necessary step in the audit as required by GAGAS. I am going to explain some elementary steps to perform the audit steps for COSO. Then, I am going to limit the discussion on internal controls to where the results of the internal control review fit into my POER methodology. I have reviewed internal controls primarily at US Customs, Regulatory Audit, so my perspective on the subject is seen through the lens of a compliance auditor for US Customs Regulatory Audit.

Basically, any internal control deficiencies noted in the review are noted in the workpapers and audit report. In the audit report, the cause and recommendations sections will reflect the internal control deficiency. In the cause section, the auditor would state the internal control deficiency and in the recommendation section the auditor would describe what needs to be done to correct the internal control deficiency, usually increased monitoring/review of the trade area reviewed, written internal control procedures, etc. As stated before, my focus is almost exclusively on finding noncompliance and Loss of Revenue and internal controls are not going to contribute much to this, other than to explain why and how the noncompliance and LOR occurred. I suggest you follow the audit program, checklists, and questionnaires, interviews with company, and review of GAGAS Yellow Book to get a good idea of the procedures to use during this internal control review. The government agency you work for should provide you the following documents/audit steps to perform your internal control review

The main function of the internal control review is that it is used in conjunction with the risk assessment to complete the sampling plan (See sampling plan chapter). The number of samples in each area chosen for review is determined to an extent by whether the auditor rates internal controls as weak, adequate, or strong. The risk assessment if rated at high, moderate, or low. The combination of these two factors determines the areas to review as well as the number of samples to be examined. If internal controls are strong and risk assessment is low, the sample size will be small for the trade area. On the other hand, if the internal controls are weak and the risk assessment is rated as high, the sample size will be large for the trade area.

These are the documents/tools you need to complete the internal control review.

Questionnaire – Find the current one to use from your government agency

Checklists for different trade areas -

Interviews with company personnel

Walkthrough – Usually during entrance conference, where the auditor documents internal controls and obtains supporting documentation from the company to verify that the internal controls actually exist.

The auditor needs to obtain documentation for the various components of internal control:

Control Environment –Management attitude towards internal control, purchasing department, contact for department, company reviews of trade areas, written internal control procedures, knowledge of regulations by staff, upper management involvement in the process. Basically, this is the overall feel/summary of department you are working with.

Risk assessment – Does company perform risk assessment on trade areas so that it can review/monitor these areas for potential non-compliances?

Control Activities –Written policies and procedures of trade areas and any documentation and other information obtained through interviews. Proper segregation of duties. Properly supervised and competent staffing in order to support compliance audit. Has management put in the resources to incorporate and maintain internal controls in areas being reviewed in compliance audit? Is there proper training of staff?

Information & Communications - Obtain information of whether departments communicate and coordinate with each other. Purchasing, receiving, accounting, etc. Are internal control problems communicated to all relevant departments to take action? Are internal control problems followed up on and resolved? Does the company inform Customs of any problems found?

Monitoring – Does company perform internal reviews of trade areas, keep scores on vendors/brokers, test and monitor trade areas? Coordinate with the government on any problems identified and submit disclosures when necessary?

Here is a summary of the audit steps to be completed for internal controls:

Internal control review – Audit results will be based on questionnaires and checklists, documentation, monitoring activities.

Workpapers – Audit program will have section for internal control. Review under separate workpaper for internal control.

Conclusion results – if deficiencies found use these as causes/recommendations to improve processes.

Audit Report – Internal controls can be in the Cause, recommendations sections of report if there are weaknesses.

Scope & Methodology of audit report, the review of internal controls is required by GAGAS

In my experience, most if not all, deficiencies in internal controls are related to

1. No written internal controls
2. Inadequate or no monitoring reviews of trade areas by management
3. Lack of training or competence of staff

In terms of monitoring, the company should be taking a sample for trade areas and performing reviews either monthly or quarterly. In order to do this, the company must have written procedures as well as perform a risk assessment of areas to look at. If the company is not performing monitoring, this deficiency will require a follow-up audit and will usually be one of the causes of the non-compliance and well as a recommendation to implement a monitoring program.

The main points to remember regarding the internal control review. Internal control review is required by GAGAS and is usually included in the audit program, if a requirement. The internal control review and risk assessment are used to select the sample based on their relative strengths or weaknesses. Any deficiencies noted in internal control must be disclosed in workpapers and audit report. The audit report section of Cause will usually include deficiencies in internal control related to lack of risk assessment and monitoring by the company and the Recommendations section will include a recommendation for the company to start performing risk assessments and monitoring trade areas that are identified as a risk area.

Chapter 3
Organizing

In martial arts especially in the internal martial arts, there is a great emphasis on being "connected". What does that mean and how do you attain this? In terms of martial arts, being connected means your whole body is connected together. For example, when you punch it is not just from your shoulder to arm. You move from your toes all the way to your waist to your shoulders to your arms. This increase the strength of the punch because it is connected from the ground all the way to the tips of your fingers instead of coming from a separate part of your body. In this way, you can weaken your adversary by separating his shoulder away from the rest of his body, so he/she can't be connected.

Using power generated from the ground is used a lot in internal martial arts like Tai Chi. It can be very powerful, and I have experienced this power in Tai Chi push hands training. A few times, I have been able to push my adversary several feet away just with my palm against their bodies as I was connected to the ground, and they were just using their shoulders and arms. The other aspect of connection is martial arts to be connected to your adversary. This means, if possible, to touch your adversary or be in contact with his body while fighting. That way you will know your adversary. Then you can neutralize and counter-attack he/she when you find their weak points. So, there are two aspects to this idea. Your body must be connected, and you must be connected to your adversary in order to predict what he is going to do so that you can neutralize and counter-attack.

In terms of audit, perhaps the most important thing you need to know about this is to connect the audit program to the workpapers. If you learn nothing else in this book, this is an incredibly important step. Without performing this step, your audits will not be connected and you will be unable to easily demonstrate that you have completed the steps in the audit program. In other words, you have not completed your compliance audit and the supervisor can send you back out to the field to complete the audit. This is the last thing in the world you would want to happen.

Basically, as in planning, organizing begins with the audit program. The auditor creates the reference number in the audit program such as (I am creating US Customs audit program as an example here):

Audit Program Step	W/P Reference
Summary	A-1
Planning	B-1
Review ACS government database	B-2
Risk Assessment	C-1
Internal Controls	D-1
Sample Selection	E-1
Evaluation of Sample	F-1
Summarize Audit results	G-1
Draft Audit Report	H-1
Finalize Audit Report	I-1
Closing Audit Steps	J-1

Notice how the audit program steps on the left are linked to workpaper references on the right side (A1 to J1). This shows the reviewer and supervisor that you completed the audit steps listed in the audit program and have workpapers (audit support) to show that you did the work!

How do you connect the audit program to the work-papers? Take the actual step in the audit program and copy it as your objective in the Purpose section of your workpaper. You can copy the actual step if it is simple and straightforward or you can modify the wording of the audit step into the objective as long as the same action is accomplished.

The information you gleam from planning data from the company database/submissions, internet research of company, tax returns prior audits, disclosures, analytical procedures, etc. must all be documented in a workpaper and if any audit leads/risks are identified carried over and linked to the risk assessment. Link planning workpaper to supporting documentation and the audit program.

The risk assessment workpaper and internal control workpaper must be linked to the sampling plan. Both these documents need to be linked to the audit program and supporting workpapers as well.

The sample evaluation and summary workpapers for each trade area reviewed must be referenced back to source documents and supporting workpapers (risk assessment, internal controls, audit leads, supporting documentation such as invoices, payments, etc. Also link to audit program to show you have performed audit step.

The audit report must be referenced/linked to summary workpapers for each trade area reviewed. Also link to audit program to show you have performed audit step.

Also document regulations which are relevant to your audit. These will be connected by putting the relevant government regulations in the Source section of workpapers and Criteria section of the audit report. This is critical if you have LOR and non-compliances in your audit.

The summary workpaper PSSC will be connected to the Results of audit section of the audit report and linked to the audit program. The scope and methodology section of the summary workpaper will include all preparatory steps, risk assessment, walkthrough, interviews internal control assessment, etc...as well as sample size and methodology. Connect all the information you used to get to the sample taken.

The Conclusion of the audit report will answer the Objective section.

I will now use an example of an outdated Drawback audit program from US Customs Regulatory Audit to provide a general example of how to connect the audit program to the workpapers.

These are actual audit steps from US Customs Regulatory Audit Drawback Audit. This document was created by US Customs Regulatory Audit. In my 18 plus years at US Customs Regulatory Audit, I did not perform a drawback audit, although I am familiar with the regulations. Some background. In US Customs terminology, Drawback is where the importer basically asks the federal government for a 99% refund and fees on imported items that are either exported out of the U.S. or destroyed. I am going to show you an example of W/P 1.1 A, planning and preparation and W/P for Audit Step 3,1.E. There are different types of drawbacks; Manufacturing, Unused, Not Confirming to Sample or Specifications (which is the one I selected Audit Step 3,1.E), and Substitution Petroleum products.

DRAWBACK AUDIT PROGRAM

TABLE OF CONTENTS

OBJECTIVE

The objective of this section is to provide reasonable assurance that the drawback claimant will be compliant with Customs laws and regulations as they relate to claimed drawback.

1.1 PLANNING AND PREPARATION

Subobjective: The subobjective of this section is to plan and prepare for the audit.

Audit Step Initials & Date W/P Ref.

A. Contact members of the drawback audit team. ______ ______

1. Request Drawback Profile from the Field Audit Specialist – Drawback ______ ______

2. Notify the Office of Investigations and obtain a TECs check to assure that the claimant is not under investigation. ______ ______

3. Based on the drawback profile, notify each drawback office where the claimant has filed claims that an audit is to be performed of this claimant's drawback program and request a suspension of claim liquidation until an audit report is issued. Since the claimants can file anywhere in the country, there may be more than one cognizant drawback office. ______ ______

4. Coordinate with the Computer Audit Specialist, Drawback Specialist, account manager and other team members as necessary. Review Drawback Specialist files. ____

I am now going to document Step 1.1 A of the Drawback audit program. You can set up either separate workpapers or one workpaper with the Purpose: Contact members of the drawback audit team. Note this is under Step 1.1 Planning in the Drawback audit Table of contents.

One workpaper could be referenced as W/P B-X-X (Planning)

Purpose: Contact members of the drawback audit team.

Source: FAS, OI, Drawback Offices in City, RAD Computer Audit Specialist

Scope/Methodology:
Requested Drawback Profile from the Field Audit Specialist – Drawback on XX/XX/2022.
Notify the Office of Investigations and obtain a TECs check to assure that the claimant is not currently under investigation
Notified drawback office where the claimant has filed claims that an audit is to be performed of this claimant's drawback program and request a suspension of claim liquidation until an audit report is issued
Coordinated with the Computer Audit Specialist, Drawback Specialist, account manager and other team members as necessary. Reviewed Drawback Specialist files.

Conclusion:
Contacted members of the Drawback Audit Team
Sam XXXX, Field Audit Specialist provided the drawback profile information to me on XX/XX/2022.
Amy XXXX, OI Agent provided TECs check to me on XX/XX/2022. There were no current investigations indicated in the TECs check.
Notified Jim XXXX of the (City) drawback office where the claimant has filed claims that an audit is to be performed of this claimant's drawback program. He/she agreed to our request for a suspension of claim liquidation until an audit report is issued.
Held a meeting with Ralph XXX, Computer Audit Specialist, Jim XXX, Drawback Specialist, Helen XXX, account manager and other team members on XX/XX/2022. (See Notes of meeting below)
Reviewed Drawback Specialist files and noted any information we may use in the files for our risk assessment.

Notes of Meeting Held on XX/XX/2022
Attendees:

Ralph XXX, Computer Audit Specialist, Jim XXX, Drawback Specialist, Helen XXX, account manager
Details of Meeting
Attendees: Ralph XXX, Computer Audit Specialist, Jim XXX, Drawback Specialist, Helen XXX, account manager
We discussed drawback.......etc.

As stated above, you could also set up a separate workpaper for each step, but that would be less efficient and repetitive but if your supervisor is slow or of dull normal intelligence, which is thankfully the exception not the rule, as most supervisors in the federal government are pretty competent, just do what he/she tells you to do.

I will now move forward to the next steps in the audit program which are noted in the following detailed audit steps below (Audit Step 3.1.E). These workpapers will still have the structure I have set up above, but you most likely will have to have more detail as they involve samples and testing and separate workpapers for each step rather than combining a relatively simple planning audit step.

E. MERCHANDISE NOT CONFORMING TO SAMPLE OR SPECIFICATIONS - 19 U.S.C. 1313(c)

OBJECTIVE: The objective is to verify that merchandise that is the subject of drawback meets the requirements of 19 U.S.C. 1313(c).

	Audit Step	Initials & Date	W/P Ref
1.	Based on the sample, verify importation, payment of duty and receipt. Verify timeline.		
2.	Determine the reason the merchandise is being exported, based on the requirements of 19 U.S.C. 1313(c): A. Not conforming to sample or specification; B. Shipped without the consent of the consignee; or C. Determined to be defective at the time of importation.		
3.	Verify that the importer and exporter are the same entity.		
4.	Determine method being used to show that the export was imported on a particular import entry, that is, no substitution is allowed.		
5.	Verify exportation of merchandise. Note that it is possible for merchandise to have been used in the U.S. Also, merchandise must be presented to Customs prior to exportation.		

This audit program step 3.1.E would then be connected to the workpaper corresponding to this audit step. I would set up a Summary and detailed workpaper: Purpose, source, scope & methodology, and conclusion with:

Summary Workpaper:
Purpose: To determine if merchandise included in the drawback claim meet the requirements of Merchandise not Conforming to Sample or Specifications

Source: Specific regulation, for Merchandise not Conforming to Sample or Specifications 19 U.S.C. 1313(c), Drawback Claim, inventory records, bills of material, manufacturing records, ACE database (imports), AES database (exports), ACE Payment Record, payment records

Scope/Methodology

1. We selected 10 samples of Merchandise not Conforming to Sample or Specifications from the drawback claim to determine if the merchandise meet the requirements of 19 U.S.C. 1313(c).
We verified that the company imported the merchandise claimed as Drawback not conforming to sample or specifications Imported – By tracing the drawback samples back to the Customs Form 7501 and importations documents, to demonstrate that the samples were imported.
We verified that the company paid the duties due for the 10 drawback samples.
Payment of Duty – By tracing sample payment amounts to US Customs CF 7501 and ACE Customs Database record which shows details of importation including duty paid.
We verified that the company received the merchandise for the 10 drawback samples.
Receipt – Tracing the samples to inventory records and receiving reports to demonstrate the merchandise was received after importation.
We verified the timeline for the 10 drawback samples.
Timeline – Verified dates of importation, receipt, payment of duty, and exportation. Verified that merchandise was exported within the timeline specified in the regulations. (Now 5 years). Exportation records obtained by reviewing Company AES record (Exports) filed with US Commerce Department.
2. We determined the reason the merchandise is being exported based on the requirements of 19 U.S.C. 1313(c) by reviewing manufacturing documents for the 10 samples. The manufacturing documents showed the items were defective, which was the reason the merchandise was exported.
3. We reviewed the importer's name and address by reviewing ACE Customs Database for imports and compared this information to the exporter name and address in the AES Commerce Database for Exports. The names and addresses matched.

4. We reviewed CF 7501 records for the 10 samples that were exported to specifically identify the merchandise was imported into U.S. No exceptions noted.
5. We reviewed records provided by the importer from the AES Commerce database that showed the 10 samples were exported. The 10 samples were not used in U.S.

Results of Audit/Conclusion: Answers the objective derived from audit program. We verified that merchandise that is the subject of manufacturing drawback meets/does not meet the requirements of 19 U.S.C. 1313(c) for merchandise not conforming to Sample or Specifications. This answers the detailed objective.
Followed by:
We found no exceptions in or sample of 10 items claimed for Drawback. or
We found X errors in our sample of 10 items claimed for Drawback with a LOR of $XX.

We would then reference this workpaper (Part 3.1 Drawback Testing Step E) related to Drawback of merchandise not Conforming to Sample or Specifications back to the audit program, sampling plan, sample evaluation, and maybe risk assessment. We would also reference this information from the audit report back to this workpaper. This workpaper would be used as a reference to support all areas of the audit report where Drawback Merchandise Not Conforming to sample or specification was mentioned/implied as part of drawback audit, Objective, Scope& Methodology, Results/Conclusion, etc.

Note that this detailed step is Step E with the overall objective being compliance with 19 U.S.C. 1313(b).

In order to write the Summary workpaper,

OBJECTIVE: The objective is to verify that merchandise that is the subject of manufacturing drawback meets the requirements of 19 U.S.C. 1313(b).

You would have to incorporate Part 3.1 Drawback Testing, Steps A to D and Steps F to complete the Summary workpaper.

I usually include a lot of details in the summary workpapers in relation to the documentation that I reviewed. For example, on the audit step, "We verified that the company paid the duty for the drawback samples." I like to include a lot of details of what I reviewed (ACE payment records, CF 7501, etc.) as this summary workpaper is hyperlinked to the detailed workpapers, so the supervisory reviewer could just go to the link and see the specifics of the documents reviewed. Otherwise, if workpaper was general and didn't explain what the auditor did, wouldn't that make it more difficult for the reviewer to understand what the auditor did and looked at? Also, the source section in the summary would be difficult to fill out if there were not enough details of the documentation reviewed. I would link/reference the summary workpaper from the documents reviewed to the spreadsheet results of review of the document in the specific workpapers as that would save time and effort.

The reviewer should not act as a private eye to try and figure out what an auditor did. More details in the summary might be somewhat repetitive, but it is easier to understand and link directly to the spreadsheet results which makes a reviewer's job easier as errors, LOR, and non-compliances is what a reviewer should focus on. If this is a clean audit with no findings, the reviewer should then focus on whether GAGAS was adhered to and whether enough was done to support this conclusion. Exceptions in my opinion, should be emphasized and focused on by the reviewer. This is why it is better to really explain things in detail.

In summary, your audit should be connected as follows:

Audit Program – linked to workpapers, audit report using workpaper referencing

Workpaper (General) – Objective from audit program carried to workpaper Purpose (objective) to show audit step was completed.

Modify if you have to but make sure your modifications don't change the desired result of the audit step. Conclusion in workpaper should answer objective. Workpapers should be connected to supporting documentation as well.

Planning Steps – create workpapers (including entrance conference), linked to source documents by workpaper reference and back to audit program, included in Scope & Methodology of audit report

Risk assessment – linked to workpaper and source documents, sampling plan and back to audit program, included in Scope & Methodology of audit report

Internal control review - linked to workpapers, source documents, sampling plan, and back to audit program, included in Scope & Methodology of audit report as well as Cause/Recommendations in the audit report, if weaknesses in internal control found.

Sampling Plan – Linked to workpapers where audit tests on samples performed and back to audit program and risk assessment, internal control review, included in Scope & Methodology of audit report

Sample evaluation workpapers - Linked to supporting documents where sample evaluation performed, and back to audit program, carried over to Results of Audit in audit report detailing errors in sample.

Results of Audit (Trade Areas) - Linked to audit planning steps, supporting workpapers where sample evaluation performed, and back to audit program, carried over to Results of Audit in audit report on whether company in compliance with regulations and any LOR found in sample for each trade area in audit report.

Summary Results of Audit (Overall Results of Audit)– Linked to Results of Audit (Trade Area) workpapers, and back to audit program, carried over to Summary Results of Audit in audit report on whether company in compliance with regulations and any LOR found in sample for all trade areas in audit report.

Exit Conference/Company response – Linked to audit program and audit report

You can see how things are interrelated. The audit program is fully referenced to workpapers and audit report which shows it was completed. The audit report is referenced to all workpapers, Risk assessment and Internal Controls are referenced to sampling plan. Sampling plan is referenced to sample evaluation workpapers. Sampling evaluation workpapers are referenced to results for audit (Trade Area) workpapers and summary results of audit workpapers and audit report results. Planning steps (entrance conference) and exit conference/company response are referenced to audit program and audit report to show they were performed.

Remember that the audit program, workpapers, and audit report must all be reviewed and signed off by your supervisor before the audit report is issued. In addition, the audit may be selected for review by Headquarters Quality Assurance teams. Therefore, it is in the auditor's best interest to demonstrate that all work was completed in a clear and concise way and hyperlinked all the way from the audit report to source documents.

An audit that is connected together is much more powerful than an audit with just separate parts. There is more focus and things fit together much better. You can support and present your evidence more clearly as the audit program, planning steps, risk assessment, internal control review, sampling plan, sample evaluation, summary results of audit workpapers, and audit report are all aligned together giving you a strong foundation from the ground to your fingers. Remember that it is critical to be able to support any non-compliances and LOR with strong supporting documentation.

Remember to Hyperlink directly to the source documents to leave no doubt that the evidence is supported in a clear, concise way. Ensure you're your referencing links go directly to the supporting documentation. Utilize bookmarks in MS Word in order to link to specific areas of documents such as a payment amount. You can also create textboxes on documents in order to provide additional explanations on your source documents. Make your referencing simple and easy to follow so that your audit supervisor can happily just click away to the end!

I have provided the following quick guide showing how various parts of the audit are connected/hyperlinked together using my POER methodology to give auditors a quick overview on connecting the dots of an audit

Connections -POER

Audit Program
Referenced to workpapers
Referenced to Audit Report
Audit Planning
Preliminary Audit Planning
Referenced to Audit Program and supporting documentation
Risk Assessment
Referenced to Audit Program and supporting documentation
Internal Control Review
Referenced to Audit Program and supporting documentation
workpapers
Sampling Plan – Referenced to risk assessment and internal control workpapers
Sample Evaluation – Referenced to supporting workpapers, Results of audit by trade area, Summary of Audit Results and Audit Report

Results of Audit by Trade Area, Cost element, asset category, etc.
Referenced to Audit Program
Referenced to Audit Planning Steps
Referenced to Source Documents
Referenced to Sampling Plan
Referenced to Sample Evaluation
Summarize Audit Results
Summary of Audit Results – Referenced to Audit Report and supporting Workpapers Results of Audit by Trade Area
Company Response – Referenced to Audit Report
Audit Report
Audit Report – Referenced to Audit Program, Audit Planning, Summary of Audit Results, supporting Workpapers, and Company Response

Chapter 4
Executing

Executing is the part of the audit where you take various sections of the audit and combine information together in order to come up with a calculation of LOR and cite any non-compliances. Basically, all the planning steps (risk assessment) and internal control review results/leads are combined in order to come up with a sample plan. The auditor then evaluates the sample and summarizes the results in the workpapers which are then summarized in an audit report.

Execution - Sampling, Testing, Evaluation requires us to actually know the adversary and where the weaknesses are. We do this by reviewing all the information we have at our disposal. We get to know the adversary by reviewing Company information, submissions, disclosures, prior audit findings, trial balance, general ledger accounts, invoices, purchase orders, shipping documentation, contract mix, Payments, bank statements etc. This then leads to the risk assessment and internal control review which results in our sampling plan and sample evaluation. The selection and evaluation of the sample can make or break a compliance audit. The compliance auditor wants to ensure that there is the greatest probability of finding non-compliances and LOR by reviewing the samples chosen. This is a critical step. Just. selecting a sample without understanding the auditee's game, is like blindly throwing a dart and hoping you will find something by hitting a bulls -eye.

If the compliance audit result is findings of non-compliance and LOR, it saves the compliance auditor a great deal of time and energy if he/she can get the company to agree to quantify LOR and agree to correct non-compliances. This will also save time and energy during the follow-up review when quantification and controls implementation to correct deficiencies will also need to be reviewed.

This section is related to the following steps:

Loss of Revenue (LOR) Calculations

Sampling Plan

Sample selection

Evaluation of sample

Summarize results of sample evaluation

Summarize results of audit – Summary workpaper from audit report

Overall Objective

As our objective is finding LOR and non-compliance with government regulations. I will start with LOR calculations as this is a really important step. You want to make absolutely sure that your LOR is correct in order for your audit to have any credibility. Asking the auditee for money is a really difficult task and most companies will do almost anything to get out of paying any significant sums of money. Therefore, you must have a good methodology of calculating LOR. I learned this method from DCAA on LOR calculations.

Here is how DCAA calculated its LOR calculation:

LOR Calculations:
DCAA (Questioned = decrease in rate and base)
Questioned rate X Proposed Base
Audit Adjusted rate X Questioned Base

The first formula takes into account adjustments to indirect pool costs for inflated estimates, unallowable, un-allocable, and unreasonable costs as well as indirect rate base adjustments applied to proposed/incurred base costs.

The second calculation take into account, adjustments due to questioned base costs. For instance, questioned direct labor due to labor rate or labor hour adjustments would be multiplied by the audit adjusted fringe benefit rate, and any questioned direct labor and fringe benefits would then be multiplied by the audit adjusted overhead rate. Finally, the questioned direct labor, fringes, and overhead would be multiplied by the audit adjusted G&A rate. These LOR calculation formulas are useful to provide information about how much LOR are due to rate adjustments and how much are due to base adjustments. These LOR calculation methodology formulas are also especially useful when there are multiple indirect rates like at DCAA.

I would also highly recommend that you check your calculations whenever using the DCAA LOR calculation methodology or on non-DCAA audits by using the following formula (Company Submission amounts minus audit adjusted amounts) to make sure you are including everything correctly as there may be audit scenarios out there where the DCAA LOR calculation methodology may not work.

Declared/reported values X declared/reported rates (Company Submission)

Minus

Audit adjusted/values X audit adjusted rates

Equals LOR

This calculation would also include any unreported value in audit adjusted amounts and declared/reported value, if auditee included.

The auditor must also be fair when calculating LOR. Disclose any instances of offsets and refunds to the auditee, if applicable. Do not ignore or exclude offsets or refunds to the customer or the auditor may be seen as unethical. If your audit has no LOR or a negative LOR, so be it and move on to the next audit. The objective is to find the really bad companies out there that are abusing the system.

How do you develop the sampling plan? Hypothetically, you combine your review of internal controls and your risk assessment as well as any pertinent information from planning steps such as analysis of company data and results of interviews/questionnaires/checklists (which you can include and reference in risk assessment to simplify things). Take all the trade areas you found to have risk in your risk assessment and utilize this information to select the sample. The sampling plan should directly reflect the risk you identified in the risk assessment and data analysis steps in planning. Areas with potential LOR and non-compliance will then be evaluated. Notice how all parts of your audit are connected with other areas.

Your sampling plan should look something like this. This example is US Customs sampling plan, which I created:

Sampling Plan

Trade Area	Risk Assessment	Internal Control Review	No. Of Samples selected
Declared Value	High	Moderate	100
Foreign Vendor Payments	High	Moderate	20
Assists	High	Moderate	20
Classification	High	Weak	100
FTA	Medium	Weak	20

Sampling Plan

Trade Area	No of Samples	Sampling Method	Basis for selection (W/P)
Declared Value	100	Statistical	Risk assessment, I/C
Foreign Vendor Payments	20	Judgmental	Risk Assess. vendor analysis, I/C
Assists	20	Judgmental	Risk Assessment, Trial Balance
Classification	100	Statistical	Risk assessment, I/C
FTA	20	Judgmental	Risk Assessment, I/C

This sampling plan explains who, what, and why the sample was selected and the methodology used which must include the risk assessment and review of internal controls. The auditor utilized the risk assessment, internal control, and other analyses from the planning steps and selected the trade area of value and classification with 100 samples as risk of noncompliance and LOR was medium to high in the risk assessment and moderate to weak internal controls. The usual suspects for value in the risk assessment are undervaluation, assists, Unreported value, related party, NDCs deductions, etc. The risk for classification is mis-classification. Statistical sampling was used versus judgmental sampling as the number of samples in the universe was too large for judgmental sampling. Judgmental samples were also selected for Unreported value (foreign vendor payments), assists, and Free Trade Agreement transactions. You can use the DCAA sampling plan (which is available to the public) on the internet to select and evaluate your sample using statistical sampling techniques. You can set up an Excel spreadsheet to set up and analyze the results of your sample. The details of the sample in the Excel spreadsheet can usually be downloaded from information in the government database or from the Company's accounting system.

When you request the samples from the auditee, do so in writing and include in the Request Worksheet. This step is actually pretty important and can help you sustain your findings if performed correctly. In the request to the company, you should include specific information about transactions of the samples selected including G/L account number, purchase order, invoice number, etc. Also ask for any supporting documentation for the transactions such as payment information, shipping information, inventory records, etc. Finally, cite the government regulation you think the company might be non-compliant with and if possible, the reason you have suspicions. This will put the company on notice that you are attacking them and you will be telling them the reasoning.

As I stated earlier, you must be completely open with the auditee throughout the audit. This is the way to test them. Expect a counter-attack or submission if the company can't get out of agreeing with your position.

When the company responds to your request, if they agree that there is a non-compliance with LOR hopefully, then more power to you. However, what if the company disagrees with your findings and the auditee tells you your position is hokey! The answer is you should have already predicted what their response was going to be during the planning stage. You should have enough knowledge to be able to challenge your adversary. You should review the company's response and based on their response and the strength of the supporting evidentiary documentation they provide you, determine if you want to drop the issue or proceed.

I usually proceed if there is a high probability of prevailing. I like the odds when they are like 65% to 70%. Make sure you run your finding through management and the customer to see what they think. An example of high probability would be the employee settlement expense in the incurred cost audit that I worked on. I went through the legal files and determined through my reading of the legal cases that the company would most likely have lost some of the cases. I questioned the employee settlement costs based on DCAA Headquarters guidance, which stated the employee settlement expense would be unallowable if the auditee were most likely to lose the legal case. The company attorney responded that I was being prejudiced on my reading of the legal cases and being too negative. This same company attorney had lambasted the previous auditor who had originally questioned the employee settlement expenses. He stated that her audit "defied logic" because she was questioning the costs without a solid basis. Based on the weakness of his response to me, the evidence I saw with my own eyes and DCAA management accepted my findings based on recent Headquarters guidance, I proceeded. Win or lose, do not live on an island with your findings. Look at every angle with the goal of winning!

Something else to consider. Don't bother your contact at the company by barging in unannounced or spending a lot of time questioning them. I was working with someone at DCAA during the incurred cost audit who would constantly check on the company contact there and inform our supervisor whenever our company contact was not at her desk. She would just barge in without an appointment and question her constantly. After a few weeks, the supervisor received a complaint and she was forbidden to have any contact with the company contact. She retired soon after that.

Bothering your contact without purpose only makes you a nuisance and you are not intimidating them by bothering them. You are not being a "badass" by doing this. The only way to truly intimidate the auditee is to outthink and outwork them on an intellectual level with questions that are difficult for them to answer because it leads to their pocketbook. I was able to work with the company contact because I only spoke to her by appointment only and I always had a reason/agenda that I would go over with her. I always appeared as a mysterious, efficient person who did not waste time. I would get right to the point with her. She told my supervisor that she liked working with me and that led to me getting the G&A portion of the Incurred Cost audit.

My point is if you do the proper planning and thinking on an audit, you don't need to badger your contact. All the work is done between your ears and you are like a real estate agent. A real estate agent could be lying on a beach in Hawaii, but if they did the work, they can sell a property while they are enjoying themselves drinking a margarita on the beach. It is all about preparation and knowing/identifying your adversary's weaknesses. Try to appear efficient and someone that doesn't waste time to the company contact and you will earn the respect from the company that a compliance auditor covets.

During the sample evaluation stage of the compliance audit, count up the number of errors for the samples that are non-compliant and be sure to calculate any LOR for the samples. Segregate the errors in the sample by type of error, payment undervaluation, related party, unreported value, assists, NDC deductions, etc. You should have Excel spreadsheets for each of the tests performed on each type of error test, and then summarize and total. Summarize the different type of errors by Trade area. Present the total number of errors and any LOR for the sample in the summary results of your workpaper and Audit Report. Show by both type of error for value and total for value and by total for classification and FTA in this example. You may also show the value of population for sample in case of any type of statistical projection for the sample, which is beyond the scope of this book, but I will mention this. Sample evaluation example below

Sample Evaluation

Trade Area	No of Samples	No, Errors	Loss of Revenue	Pop. Value
Declared Value	100	4	$30.10	$10,000,000
Foreign Vendor	20	2	500.00	
Payments				
Assists	20	0	0	
Classification	100	12	330.16	10,000,000
FTA	20	1	50.12	

To get the LOR calculation, calculate what was declared for the tariff rate and declared unit price and quantity (dollar value) and any declared unreported value and compare to the audit adjusted tariff rate and audit adjusted unit price and quantity (dollar value) and any audit adjusted unreported value for the sampled items reviewed. At this point, get the auditee to agree to quantify LOR judgmental samples or perform a statistical sample projection using DCAA's statistical sampling program available online.

When you get the results of audit for all trade areas (number of errors in the sample); make sure to summarize the errors by trade area into a Summary of Audit Results workpaper. Then, it is critical that you keep the company informed of any findings you have throughout the audit. At this stage, try to get the company to agree to the findings and to quantify the LOR before you start on your audit report. Get the company's agreement in writing. This will make your life simpler as well as confirm your assumptions. This is the crucible or true test of your skills as an auditor. Your evidence and position should be overwhelming and you should speak to the company in a scientific, objective way and get them to come to the same conclusion. All your facts and figures should be organized and you will be in control using the POER method.

Other Considerations/Insights in the Execution of your compliance audit

Never do anything that will make the auditee or your management question your integrity or your sanity. At DCAA, I met a person whose greatest achievement was going through a garbage can and finding fraud at a defense contractor. I spoke to him many times before he retired. He had a twisted mind and always accused the companies he audited of committing fraud without any evidence. He was auditing at the time I started at DCAA but shortly afterward was put into an administrative job.

Even if this person had the information from the garbage can, he could not use it as the company did not provide him this information or verify whether it was real or not. He also set a bad precedent for future auditors as the company would accuse DCAA of playing "dirty pool". The only information you can utilize as a compliance auditor must be honestly requested by the compliance auditor based on a plan and audit program. You must be open and honest with the auditee.

I have noticed throughout my career that a lot of auditors were promoted to management very quickly. Many of them did not have the opportunity to perform many audits. Some only worked on one to two audits their whole career, before becoming a supervisor and reviewing audits. Others went into headquarters doing a lot of administrative work. There was no place for an auditor like me that got great audit results because that was not the criteria for getting ahead in the federal government. Instead, politics and race, were the main determinant of promotions. The result of this was a lot of auditors in management did not like to look at the "dirty" details and try to understand the underlying mechanics of the audit. They certainly did not try to outthink, outwork, and outhustle the auditee. They were afraid to get their hands "dirty" and avoided doing detailed reviews of audit findings that were difficult to comprehend without a lot of field experience.

I recommend that audit agencies send these people back to the field to perform audits as this is the only way to actually improve audit skills. This would also help with some of the audit planning and workload as more audits would get done. In order to be able to execute either as a compliance auditor or supervisory reviewer, you must actually be able to perform an audit. This sounds simple, but you would be surprised at the number of audit supervisors who would be unable to do so. If they can't do an audit after so many years of inactivity, they can use my POER methodology to enable them to survive an audit!

A lot of auditors can talk a good game especially when they are supervisors or managers who don't perform audits but unless they can actually successfully complete an audit. What else would give them credibility.? How can someone review another person's audit, if they have performed few or no successful audits themselves? As I explained earlier, unless you can perform an audit and find significant LOR and non-compliances if they exist, then that is the crucible of gung fu auditing. A supervisor auditor is crossing t's and dotting I's unless he/she can perform a solid risk assessment and perform proper planning, organizing, and reporting. Auditing for results takes a singular purpose and the only real way to be good at compliance auditing to actually find LOR and non-compliances by going out to the field!

Throughout my career, I have been willing to go mano a mano and put it all on the line with hundreds of companies and I have been able to get LOR and non-compliances on the majority of the audits that I felt held a lot of risk. I was almost always alone and willing to put my reputation and credibility on the line every time. Unless, you're willing to do that, you should just quit and find employment elsewhere. This is not a career for the passive or meek. You must be a warrior willing to fight your way through from beginning to end with no help, other than my POER training. The only thing that matters in compliance audits is results and anybody that will tell you any different doesn't know anything! The whole organization must be one in objective and spirit if it is to succeed in its great mission.

If I can do it with all the baggage I have carried throughout my career, then you can to! Even though I found more LOR and non-compliances than any other auditor at both DCAA and Customs, I was never promoted beyond a GS-12 mainly because nobody would recognize my POER methodology. Government is politics! The people that blow their own horn over non-results get all the glory. The good thing that came out of all this is the fact that I wouldn't "polish the apple" to management and they never promoted me, which enabled me to continue improving my audit skills which have led me to creation of the POER methodology. Otherwise, I might have been promoted into management and stopped auditing out in the field.

Having worked in the federal government for 31 years, 29 years in the field. I must bring up the subject of budgets. At DCAA, the budgets could be as low as 8 hours for an assignment to a few hundred hours for larger more important assignments. At US Customs, the budgets could be in the hundreds to the thousands of hours for an assignment. How do you complete your assignments under or at budget?

The answer is having a proper audit objective, planning steps, following audit program, a good risk assessment, etc. Wait, the answer then is following my POER methodology! Not only will you be able to focus on what you need to achieve, the bonus is you will also be able to do it efficiently under budget or close to budgeted hours. Make no mistake about it, I have seen many auditors at DCAA fired for not meeting budget hours.

Scientifically, really think about cause and effect, see further than the present, if I do this what will happen in the future. If the company answers this way, how will I react or if the company can't provide requested documents. What do you do! Attack. Think ahead and when you can predict the various outcomes of different situations, then you have reached the very top of the compliance audit crop. A chess game between you and the company. Cover every angle. What is it going to take to succeed and win the battle? What documents do I need to crush the adversary? How can I move forward on this audit? This is how a fight in martial arts is won or lost. The martial artist who is properly trained and can think ahead and feel what his adversary is about to do usually wins. You attack his weak points and separate his body parts (strengths). If you can reach this level as a compliance auditor, then you can claim the title, master.

Outthink outmaneuver your adversary and predict his every move and already counteract and counterattack, then you have reached the highest level. Think Robert Downey and Sherlock Holmes where he dissects the other fighter in 3D graphic cartoons.

You must also use this talent when you select what areas you plan to review and which general ledger accounts you want to review as well as which specific transactions to select. If I review/select this account/item what effect would that possibly have on LOR/non-compliances. If it is not material or has a low probability of getting a result or if it is material and has a high probability of getting a result, you have to be able to make those predictions seeing in the future, looking ahead to cause and effect like a scientist. If you have a good plan and are thinking like a scientist about audit cause and effect, you will surely achieve a better result than just thinking in the moment or following someone else's audit. Always consider your adversary and don't underestimate him/her. Focus on the benefits/profits your adversary wants to get. Follow the adversary, match his every move and when the right time comes exploit his weakness and overcome him. Do not use strength, use your mind and training in POER.

As long as you have adequately planned, organized, executed, and reported the audit with a martial spirit, you have given yourself the best chance of winning. So, you can't control the results. When you get to the sample evaluation and results of audit, honorably accept whatever you have found. Win or lose, you let your training and practice take over. In Tai Chi, Jiu Jitsu and auditing, I used every experience as a learning experience to improve my skills and winning or losing didn't matter all that much to me. Especially in Jiu Jitsu, you learn so much by losing. Having a sweaty guy or girl get you in a chokehold after rolling all over the place can teach you so much about yourself and your breaking point. You also learn in a hurry how to improve in order to avoid this at all costs. Remember that the purpose of POER and having a marital spirit is to significantly improve your probability of winning by overwhelming your adversary on an intellectual level.

I would sometimes experience a brief happiness when the audit outcome was good and I wouldn't feel bad if no findings came up. I learned a lot about myself in this way and isn't that what life is all about? Finding yourself and the effort and sacrifice you are willing to make to try to become and audit master and improve your skills. What more can you ask for? Go into an audit with a mindset of doing everything to win and don't care about the final results. You will find yourself in the process. Learn from your mistakes and don't ever make the same mistake twice. Constantly try to improve your skills no matter the outcome.

Always conduct yourself in a professional, objective manner. Don't be arrogant, unfriendly, or negative. Use humor, scientific approach and give respect to your adversary. Everyone at the company has an education, training, and experience. Don't hold yourself above them. Think of every person as an equal. Never be racist and judge people by their merit. That is the way. Always try to be the better person even if the other side is unprofessional or mean to you. Think of yourself as Albert Einstein working on his formulas. Don't let the company get under your skin. The bad ones will try to distract you and take your focus away from your objective. Don't fall for such cheap tawdry tricks. Be prepared for war, but have a plan for the peace.
Always be objective. If your evidence/support is stronger than your adversary, you will prevail. Always keep this philosophy in your mind.

In order to execute compliance audits properly, auditors should be trained to look for areas where there have been significant valid findings in prior audits.

That is why I am recommending trainers of compliance audits at different agencies give the beginning auditor quick lists of previous material findings and LOR from previous audits. That way the beginning auditor can have an idea on how to find the game the company is playing and where the illicit profits are. For example, and I am picking this agency out of thin air, HHS/Medicare audit training staff could put together a quick list of prior audit findings with details of miscoding schemes, medical work that was not performed, overbilling, etc., so that auditors can have an idea of what to look for or if they run across a similar situation, they will know how to react.

Lastly, I will discuss an issue that is dear to all of our hearts. How to get things done efficiently and effectively. The answer is simple and prevents so many compliance auditors from performing at a high level. Stop/don't procrastinate! When information is received from the company, don't just let it sit there, incorporate the information into your audit, hyperlink it, see how it effects other parts of your audit. You stay on top on your budgets by keeping ahead. I was always able to complete audits way before schedule because once information was received, it was like a cog in a machine or crossword puzzle and I would incorporate it right away. Try to do things right away without excuses. Do not procrastinate, as the longer you do this the farther behind you will get. Execute right away. Work in an organized, effective way. Go step by step.

It's like learning ballroom dancing, do it step by step and soon enough, you will learn the whole thing. Try not to get distracted and focus, like a martial artist. Keep trying to improve your skills. Nothing comes easy in this world. It must be earned through hard work. You must be disciplined. With proper planning and my POER method, you must believe that you can meet/beat the budget in time and hours and immediately work on your audit when information comes and that will eventually lead to significant findings in the audit.

The other thing is if your supervisor asks you to do something, do not put it off! If you are still on probation, this could cost you everything. Try to finish and turn in whatever they ask you on time or early. That way you can get along with almost any supervisor no matter their personality quirks. Strike right away with a purpose and as long as you can see your goal ahead of you, you will succeed!
Procrastination/laziness is the death knell for a compliance audit! Avoid doing this at all costs.

Never give up and continue trying to learn and improve yourself throughout your career. We need every compliance auditor in this country to perform at a high level, if this country is ever to have a chance of raising revenue to reduce the burgeoning budget deficits, we are facing in this country. Do not think of your job as a paycheck. Try to think of it as a compliance auditor is upholding/protecting the revenue of the US and is very important to the national security of this country. I hope this helps to motivate all of you in this great mission!

Chapter 5
Report

I remember a class I attended while at DCAA. The class was asked a question. What is more important, workpapers or the audit report? I answered audit report and I was correct. I was asked to explain and I responded that the report is what the customer receives from DCAA. No one is going to look at work-papers unless quality assurance selects it for review or the audit goes to court. I was correct. The report is the final product and even if your workpapers are mediocre, at a minimum, your report must be good. Great if you can reach this level. The customer needs your report to be great so that he can take it to the company and beat them over the head with all your great findings and evidence to back it up.

If the goal is to get money from these people and identify non-compliances, then you must use the audit report as a battering ram. I have reviewed many audit reports at both DCAA and US Customs Regulatory Audit as a reviewer and as quality assurance and most were pretty mediocre to badly written. But once in a long while something would catch my eye. A report that was simple and direct. A report which got right to the point and focused on objective. It was very satisfying when this occurred.

I feel very strongly that the better and more detailed your workpapers are by osmosis the better your audit report will be. If you are connected and use my POER methodology, automatically, your report will be organized and will supported. You just need to make it simple, concise, and direct. The audit report represents the "end game" of your audit. The final conflict or culmination of your fight with the adversary. If your audit was well planned, organized, and executed, the job of the audit report will be made much easier for you. This is where the rubber hits the road and you must pull out all the stops.

All the details/evidence/support must come out of the word work to support your findings. You must have solid evidence like bank statements, shipping documents, copy of advertisement, invoices, etc. to support your audit report as your adversary will counter attack you for sure! Never underestimate the importance of the audit report. Just visualize yourself in a boxing match where you knock the other boxer out with one punch! Or in an MMA fight, where you get the other guy in a guillotine choke! That is what you want to achieve!

Audit Report

First thing you should do is find out if there are pro-forma reports you can use created by your agency's headquarters. created by your headquarters in your government agency. The pro-forma audit report is usually located in a database or MS Word or Excel files. However, be careful as sometimes these reports are not updated or correct. Make sure you use the most updated version. You may need to make edits to the report to get it right.

How do you know what is correct? The GAO yellow book. Read this book and utilize it to determine if all elements and language of report are correct. The pro-forma report will usually be a "shell" or bare bones example and the auditor must fill in the details but it is the place to start if there is one.

You can also use prior audit reports with the same areas audited, but you must be careful. Make sure you are comparing the prior audit reports to the pro-forma audit reports and GAO Yellow Book to make sure it is correct. Also, check header and footers, company name to make sure you change to the company you are currently auditing. Remember, take what is useful and reject what is not!

In terms of writing the audit report, Get to the point immediately! Tell the reader in simplest, concise, clearest terms what you as an auditor representing the government did and what you found and whether the company was compliant and if there is LOR.

Simplicity is crucial! Get directly to the point. Think about objective, LOR, noncompliance and all the support/evidence you have in order to topple your adversary. Don't use complicated or technical language, start with simple sentence structure to explain follow the money. Run downhill as a running back from A to Z in order. Don't juke or run side to side. Once you decide to move, just move!

Use plain simple language, start sentence from beginning to end. I have noticed many auditors do not do this but start at the middle of the sentence and work backwards and forwards. Do not do this, it is totally confusing. Ensure that there is a subject in your sentences.
An example:

We found 10 errors in our sample of 100 which resulted in LOR of $1,024. Our review of invoices, payment records, bank statements, and shipping documents disclosed, XXX company transshipped the product from China to Vietnam in order to avoid paying Anti-dumping in non-compliance with 19 CFR.351.211, 19 CFR351.212. We traced the payment and bank statement records to several vendors in China.

Versus

Through a review of documents, XXX company transshipped products through a different country (Vietnam) to avoid paying anti-dumping duties for products originating from China, which are subject to anti-dumping duties. XXX company did not declare or pay anti-dumping duties on their CF 7501. This is in non-compliance with the regulations. The company insisted the products originated in Vietnam. The company's internal controls were not adequate to prevent these errors. The quantification of the LOR related to the samples resulted in $1,024 owed to the government. Of the 100 samples reviewed, there were 10 errors found in the trade area reviewed by the auditor.

The shorter explanation the better, show things in order of importance/occurrence, step by step. Pretend you are a scientist working on an experiment, when the scientist documents the experiment, they have to do so step by step. Anything out of order and the experiment won't work, right? Plus, it makes more sense to the reader this way.

Make sure your objective in the audit report matches your workpapers and audit program. Cite relevant government regulations in the Criteria and Results of audit sections of the audit report that you derived from the summary of audit results work-paper. Unless you can cite a government regulation, you may not have a valid audit finding.

Logically explain the process in order (planning steps, risk assessment, internal controls, sampling plan) you used to find the noncompliance and LOR in the scope & methodology section of the audit report. Also, state clearly the number of errors found in the sample reviewed and any LOR for the sample in Summary of audit results and cite any internal control deficiencies found in the cause and recommendations sections of the audit report.

Make sure the auditor is the subject of the sentence. The sentence should always start with a subject (the auditor) and then the rest of the sentence (predicate) should follow. This indicates action on the part of the auditor versus just stating random facts.

Also, I like to specify the documents I reviewed. This could be useful when the company disagrees with your findings, as they will know what documents the auditor is using to attack and will usually counter-attack when the auditee thinks the auditor's specific documentation is weak or unclear. In this case with payments and bank statements, the evidence is very strong. Payments are like a brick wall to the auditee as they are difficult to excuse away as an error as to who/where the funds went to, because it involves money!

The auditor should have already shown and discussed the documentation used to support the findings in the audit report with the auditee, at the same time the auditor made the decision to question the documentation and there was a finding of non-compliance during the workpaper stage of the audit. At the time of the audit report, both parties should know everything that is going on. If there is a disagreement on the findings, the auditor must make a judgment on the strength of his evidence/support with the approval of management. If there is a high probability of winning, I would purse the finding unless there is a misunderstanding or error on the part of the auditor, which will be pointed out by the auditee at this stage.

The different sections of the report are populated primarily from your workpapers which are derived from your audit program and risk assessment. Note the connectedness. You will hyperlink your draft report to your workpapers and your workpapers will be hyperlinked to source documents. The audit program will be linked to your workpapers. Your risk assessment and internal control review will also be linked to your workpapers and audit report.

The various sections of a compliance audit report are:

Objective – Overall objective from audit report – What are the areas that you have chosen for review - derived from audit program, risk assessment, purpose section of workpapers

Criteria – Government regulations related to areas you have selected for review - derived from audit program, risk assessment, planning steps related to objective, source sections of workpapers

Scope & Methodology
These are the steps you took to complete the audit fieldwork. Derived from audit program, scope & methodology workpapers.
Be sure to state whether your audit was performed in accordance with GAGAS. Also, state whether you reviewed internal controls. This is included in the scope & methodology section of the audit report.

Results of Audit Sample evaluation results
Derived from Summary of audit results workpaper and summary workpapers for each of the trade areas reviewed. Note non-compliance and LOR here for each trade area.

Conclusion Answers objective, comply with regulations and LOR. Derived from Conclusion section of workpapers for each trade area. Note non- compliance and LOR here in total for audit.

Cause: Internal controls weaknesses noted, lack of management review, monitoring derived from internal control review workpaper.

Effect – LOR, get company to quantify LOR or if you must use a statistical projection however, a statistical projection is difficult to understand, especially precision. Effect (LOR) is derived from conclusion sections of workpapers.

Recommendations:
Compliance auditor creates recommendations based on the causes of the errors found. Usually includes internal control deficiencies as well.

Company Response/Auditor Response, if needed. If you must respond to the company, make sure you do it in an objective, scientific way with lots of evidence and audit support for the non-compliance and LOR in your audit report. Respond to every point made by the company and shoot it down the best you can. If you have properly prepared using POER, you will hopefully prevail.

Some General Thoughts/Advice on writing a compliance audit report

Refer to GAGAS Yellow Book follow this. Performance audits – Chapter 9 for information on audit reports

Always try to start off and use a subject in your sentences. We performed, we calculated, in our sample of x items, we found. Everything related to action and result with a purpose in mind. Reader must be persuaded you are in control.

Make sure to reference your audit report back to the workpapers and reference from the audit program to the report for steps related to audit report. At DCAA and US Customs, we would hyperlink the audit report back to the workpapers in the draft audit reports. In the final reviewed audit report, we would remove the hyperlinks for signature by the Field Director.

Try not to include extra information about possible or potential problems unless absolutely necessary. Focus on non-compliances and LOR for the specific areas reviewed. You could put this type of information in Other Matters to be Reported but if the area doesn't have a lot of LOR potential now or in the future, I would most likely ignore it.

Always include information and write for the reader/customer. Compliance auditing is a customer focused vocation. Never forget that. Always be courteous to your customers at meetings and never take a condescending attitude. That is the worst thing you can do is act like a Mr. Know it all. Always stay humble like Sylvester Stallone in the movie, "Rocky". Always use language that is simple and direct and is to the level of the customer reading the report. The goal of the audit report is to get the customer to take action based on our report. Basically, grab the money out of the auditee's hands and get them to correct the deficiencies so that it doesn't happen again.

This is one of the differences between a compliance audit and a financial audit. In a compliance audit, the auditor has a customer. Usually the government agency that requested the audit. The auditor also has an adversarial relationship with the auditee. This means there are ethics involved. You shouldn't accept gifts or free lunches from auditee.

In a financial audit, there is no customer requesting the audit or government agency involved and reports are read by the investing community, lenders, and regulatory agencies like SEC and other interested parties, so it can be as complex and complete as the CPA firm wants it to be. The auditor is not in an adversarial relationship and many times the CPA firm has consulting and tax business with the same company, so they are a vendor/contractor and auditee at the same time. To me this difference blurs the lines between compliance audits and financial audits.

I never worried in my career if the auditee was not happy with the results I came up with. A CPA doing a financial audit, might worry about bringing up material misstatements if the firm had a lot of other business going on with the same company. That is why I consider the compliance audit to be a form of a "pure" audit" unfettered by any constraints other than GAGAS and audit management. If the IRS and US Customs can auction assets on the internet, the federal government is pretty much all powerful.

The report is where the rubber hits the road and is the only thing that the outside world sees, unless your workpapers are subpoenaed and used in court, which doesn't happen often. Show your best face. Make your customer happy and the report easy to follow which will lead to victory.

Always keep a good relationship with your customer/requestor and inform him/her of progress throughout audit. Invite customer/requestor to meetings and the entrance and exit conference. Consult with them if any findings or LOR come up during the audit. Get them to agree to your audit results. This is needed before, during, and after the audit report is issued.

Write your report with the customer in mind. Make it easy for him/her to make a decision based on your audit report. Your job is to convince the customer to take action based on your report. Mainly, collect the revenue! Convince the reader of the superiority of your planning and the great risk assessment that you did. The excellent documentation source documents you obtained from the company to back up your findings. The clear concise language and explanations in your report and the professional meetings and presentations you had with the customer and the company.

Outthink your adversary at every turn. Have a better and stronger argument based on your cause and effect thinking. Outdraw him before he shoots you. Do not pick weak positions or issues you have a low probability of winning as that will draw away from your strength and credibility.

After sample evaluation, only include in your report findings backed by strong evidence and positions on LOR and non-compliances and drop the weaker issues with immaterial LOR. In an audit report, it is better to win all your significant material issues than win and lose issues with material and immaterial impacts as that takes its toll on your credibility. Get your management to focus/concentrate on strong findings with evidence rather than going after anything that might be wrong at a company. Win the big games like the NFC/AFC Championships and Super Bowl and lose games 16 or 17, when you have already made the playoffs.

You must conserve energy in martial arts or you will wear yourself out. This is fundamental to Jiu Jitsu. If you use up all your energy you will get choked out. In order to avoid this, you have to be smarter than your adversary and use your training. This is similar to auditing.

Conserve energy by focusing on what's important and not wasting time on creating beautiful workpapers or worksheets or wrongly thinking you have findings without verifying with the company or evaluating your evidence or wasting time in general. Write your audit report with the customer in mind so he can support your findings.

Build your audit report from your summary workpapers so all information is aligned/connected. Hyperlink/reference audit report back to support. Be sure you are able to cite a government regulation for any non-compliance noted. Working in auditing is like a marathon. There will always be other audits. Don't burn yourself out. Work smarter not harder. Spending a lot of effort on sample evaluation hoping to get findings is not efficient. Proper planning, risk assessment, and knowing the company and staying ahead of them by predicting where the significant risks are will work out a lot better for you. You must take a bigger picture of the auditing process and not rely on the results just coming because you happened to pull a sample that had noncompliance or LOR. All this should have been known beforehand. Be able to predict the next moves of your adversary to reach the highest level. Don't rely on luck or incompetence on the part of your adversary. That is the recipe for losing.

I highly recommend in the recruiting of new auditors that being able to write college thesis papers on different subjects become part of the criteria for getting hired as an auditor. This is extremely important and has helped me immensely in my career as a compliance auditor. Being able to read and write thesis papers in college will prepare new auditors read the regulations and understand them as well as write up workpapers and audit reports. Also, as a supervisor and upper management, it helps in review of audit reports.

Learning how write thesis papers in high school and college really helped me tremendously in my compliance audit career in the federal government. The reasoning and supporting facts/thesis with evidence really helps prepares you for the auditing field. It teaches focus and objective really well and prepares auditors to write reports and workpapers in an organized effective way.

I remember a Political Science class at Fresno City College taught by a professor with a crew cut. He was really intimidating and he only knew me from the one time I arrived in class late and he stopped the class and called me out to point me out as late. Later, I was the only one in the class of about 200 students who was able to write a paper on one of our US political parties dissolving itself to form a new party in order to win at the beginning of the 20th century. He was shocked when I stood up when he called the name Phillip Lee after he stated only one person in the class understood the material. I remember him say, "You're Phillip Lee?". I am not writing this to brag about my past but to point out that these classes really helped me to see through the morass of words and pick out the important points by reading and organizing thoughts in an organized way really helped me in audit.

The evidence must support the thesis. This is great training for audits and should be emphasized by trainers.

Recruiters/trainers need to spend more focus on this area of learning. You can really learn about focus. I learned so much from my teachers during my high school years at Roosevelt High School in Fresno and Fresno City College which helped me so much in my auditing career. It really prepared me to keep focus on what I was trying to do and had a great impact on my POER methodology. Without this mental training, I could have never reached this point.

Chapter 6
Follow-up Compliance Audit Review

I am devoting a separate chapter on follow-up compliance audits as they are quite common at US Customs Regulatory Audit. Follow-up audits are performed after an initial compliance audit finds deficiencies and/or LOR. The follow-up is performed in order to determine if the contractor is now in compliance with government regulations and has corrected the deficiencies noted in the audit report, and whether the auditee has quantified the LOR, as it agreed to do, correctly. In addition, this is a good way to combine the POER method in an example audit. I will combine all strategies in this follow-up audit.

Here are the general steps:

Review the following: Company submission, ACE reports, prior audit including the workpapers and audit report, disclosures, audit program. Confirm what is disclosed by tracing back to the source documents. Risk and focus should be on areas the company has not disclosed. Attack enemy's weakness not strength, known versus what is not known.

Hold entrance conference, complete risk assessment, internal control review (if necessary). Complete sampling plan, sample evaluation, summarize audit results, draft audit report, finalize audit report, closing steps.

Connect audit planning steps, program, workpapers, audit report by referencing/hyperlinking.

Communicate with customer and auditee on all phases of audit, entrance conference through the exit conference.

Here are some detailed steps to use on follow-up audit:

The Purpose/Objective to be used on workpapers and audit report: To follow-up on disclosed non-compliances and to verify LOR was quantified correctly

Focus on disclosed non-compliances. Do not look at other trade areas unless new audit lead/risk and management approves. Otherwise, avoid audit creep.

Audit Program – Usually generic in nature. Auditor must revise to suit needs of follow-up audit. Usually, tailor to include the trade areas identified in prior audit.

Prior Audit – Review prior audit to get understanding of issues. The company will usually quantify the LOR and present evidence that it has corrected any deficiencies noted based on our recommendations.

Disclosures - Look at what disclosed and unreported. Verify accuracy (math calculations of LOR) and completeness of disclosure by comparing to government databases, etc.

Do not audit creep as follow-up must answer whether company complies and has corrected deficiencies in internal controls. Usually don't look at other areas not included in original audit report.

Use information for planning detailed in Chapter on planning to re-familiarize yourself with any trade areas you may have forgotten.

Risk assessment should be based on following up on deficiencies identified. Any additional risks identified must be approved by

Supervisor before proceeding. I usually review the same trade areas for items not disclosed in the submission identified in the prior review.

An example of this is as shown:

Suppose the prior US Customs audit identified classifications of electronic imports that were misclassified and not complying with Harmonized Tariff Code and there was LOR as the correct tariff code had a duty rate while the declared tariff code did not. This was determined by the Import Specialist. US Customs auditors work with Import Specialists who determine correct HTSUS codes.

The misclassification was as shown:

Electrical Machinery and Equipment Chapter 85
Flat Panel Display Monitors 8524

Declared HTSUS code	8524.11.90.00
Duty Rate	No
Correct HTSUS code	8524.91.90.00
Duty Rate	4.5%

Although, this is not a great audit situation as probability of finding significant LOR is not high for electronic products as most electronic products are duty free, I would maximize the probability of finding LOR or non-compliance by selecting other similar tariff codes declared with no duty and see if this results in any findings. Make the most out of nothing. You could also take a statistical sample of tariff codes with no duty. The import specialist will perform the review of classification, so the auditor does not need any knowledge of the product specifications, although it wouldn't hurt to know something through research. Also, make sure you cite 19 CFR 152.11 as the relevant government regulation especially if you have LOR and non-compliances.

If there are discrepancies in value, there is more opportunity here. You can look for unreported value, perform vendor payment analysis, review general ledger for assists/unreported value, etc.

Also; If there was a finding of Anti-dumping in prior audit on products from China, I would look to see what HTSUS and was declared and choose similar tariff codes with no ADD or duty declared. This maximizes the probability of finding something in virgin territory so to speak rather than focusing on items that have been declared as subject to ADD. That is where the auditee is strong. Attack where he is weak and there is opportunity to get LOR and non-compliances. I would check the invoice, receiving report, inventory records and look for discrepancies in country of origin of imported similar items with no ADD or duty disclosed. I would be more careful of countries in Asia where the goods could be transshipped like Singapore or Vietnam. I would also check payments, vendor locations, bank statements to verify the goods did not originate from China. Note that bank statements don't lie. They are like a brick wall for the company as to who/where the payments went to.

The invoice, receiving report, general ledger, inventory record can all be manipulated with wrong country of origin, but where money goes is difficult to fabricate. In addition, the vendor in Singapore and Vietnam may have connections to a Chinese company which would be a red flag. You can also identify undervaluation if payments to the vendor are greater than what is declared.

There is also a lot of risk in FTA. This is kind of opposite thinking from ADD. In the case of FTA, the company would submit false claims related to a country that qualifies for FTA. You would need to check manufacturing records (must meet a certain percentage in Country of Origin to qualify), country of origin certificates, invoices, shipping documents, inventory records to verify the country of origin. In addition, trace to payments/bank statements and check the addresses of the vendors. If the vendor is not located in the FTA country, a red flag should come up. Just like in ADD, payments are more difficult to obfuscate. The company can fake shipping, documents, etc. There is less concern of undervaluation and misclassification as the whole transaction would be phony, so these schemes would not need to be used.

Research relevant government regulations involved with the trade area you are auditing and make sure to cite government regulations associated with any non-compliance you find.

Review internal controls if required. Under a follow-up audit, review internal controls to determine if company has fixed problems utilizing audit recommendations and improved internal control processes for trade areas found to be deficient in original audit.

Write workpapers with the objective of following up on non-compliances and verifying LOR quantification. Make sure all workpapers are referenced to source documents and support. Use purpose, source, scope & methodology, and conclusion format in your workpapers. It is critical to reference through hyperlinks (connect) audit program to risk assessment, internal controls, sampling plan, and other relevant workpapers for trade areas reviewed in follow-up. Also be sure to use bookmarks and textboxes to provide explanations.

Results of Audit (Summary) Audit Workpaper example:

Purpose: To follow-up on non-compliances noted in trade area of Value and to verify LOR quantification for adequacy and accuracy

Source: Prior audit Report XXX-XXXXXX, 19 CFR 152.103, Company XXX disclosure/LOR quantification, Compliance improvement plan, risk assessment, sampling plan, sample evaluation, payment records, bank statements, general ledger accounts, invoices.

Scope/Methodology:
We reviewed prior audit report to determine the non-compliances/deficiencies cited in audit Report XXX-XXXXXX and LOR.

We reviewed Company XXX Compliance Improvement Plan, prior disclosure and LOR quantification to determine adequacy and accuracy of submissions.

We performed a risk assessment and reviewed internal controls.

We developed a sampling plan based on the risk assessment and review of internal controls.

We selected a judgmental sample of 10 items for declared value and 10 sample items for unreported value to determine if Company XXX has corrected the non-compliances identified and quantified LOR.

We reviewed CF 7501, invoices, payment records, and bank statements for declared value and general ledger accounts for unreported value by tracing to the invoices and supporting documentation for accounts selected.

Results of Audit/Conclusion:
We found no errors in our sample of 20 sample items (10 declared value and 10 unreported value).
Audit report should also be focused on concluding the results of your follow-up review.

If there are no findings, the conclusion would be
Our audit disclosed Company XXX has corrected the deficiencies identified in prior audit XXX-XXXXXX in the trade area of value. We did not identify any additional LOR.

If there are findings, conclusion would be,
We found 1 error in our sample of 10 items in the area of unreported value. Our review of 10 sample items in declared value disclosed no errors. Company XXX is in non-compliance with 19 CFR.152.103 (x)(x). This resulted in LOR of $50. The company made additional payments to the vendor that were not reported to US Customs. Company XXX needs to quantify the LOR and provide a compliance

improvement plan on how the company plans to correct the non-compliance.

Example of Follow-up audit report on trade area of value

Audit report

Objective

Pretty much the same as purpose in Results of Audit workpaper/Conclusion and audit program. The objective is answered by the conclusion. This is how connected works.
To follow-up on non-compliances noted in trade area of Value and to verify LOR quantification for adequacy and accuracy

Criteria: 19 152.103(x)(x)

Scope & Methodology

State type of audit performed
State whether audit was performed in accordance with GAGAS
State whether Internal Control review was performed
Planning steps
Risk Assessment
Any other audit procedures performed

Sampling Plan

Example:

We selected a judgmental sample of 10 items for declared value and 10 sample items for unreported value to determine if Company XXX has corrected the non-compliances identified and quantified LOR.

This section includes the records reviewed for the trade area. We reviewed CF 7501, invoices, payment records, and bank statements for declared value and general ledger accounts for unreported value by tracing to the invoices and supporting documentation for accounts selected.

Sample Evaluation
Prepared audit report

Results of Audit: Summarizes sample evaluation and Results of Audit workpaper for trade area. Include a summary schedule of all trade areas with footnotes, if necessary.

If there are no findings, the conclusion would be:
Our audit disclosed Company XXX has corrected the deficiencies identified in prior audit XXX-XXXXXX in the trade area of value. We did not identify any additional LOR. We found no errors in our review of 10 declared value samples and 10 unreported value samples.

If there are findings, the conclusion would be:
Our audit disclosed Company XXX has not corrected the deficiencies identified in the prior audit XXX-XXXXXX in the trade area of value. Our review of 10 sample items in declared value disclosed no errors. We found 1 error in our sample of 10 items in the area of unreported value. Our review of 10 sample items in declared value disclosed no errors. Company XXX is in non-compliance with 19 CFR.152.103 (x)(x). This resulted in LOR of $50. The company made additional payments to the vendor that were not reported to US Customs. Company XXX needs to quantify the LOR and provide a compliance improvement plan on how the company plans to correct the non-compliance.

Cause: This is where the idea of connectedness comes in. If there are findings, then the reason was the CIP and internal controls were not effective in correcting the deficiencies identified in the prior audit. So, the results of the review of CIP and internal controls conclusion is placed here.

Effect
This is where you put any LOR from your Results of Audit workpaper. In the example above, this resulted in no LOR or $50. Request company to quantify LOR for trade area of value.

Recommendations:
Recommendations come from review of the CIP for anything missing or any weaknesses noted and from the review of internal controls

Company Response
Attach a copy of the company's response. Hopefully, you would have received the company's agreement with your findings. That is the holy grail of compliance auditing. This makes your life simple.

Conclusion: State whether the trade area(s) are in compliance and if the company has/hasn't corrected the deficiencies cited in prior audit and if there is LOR. This is also from Results of Audit workpaper based on results from review of sample items. Answers audit objective. Connectedness!

Final Thoughts on Audit Report

Consult GAGAS Yellow book and any Agency pro-forma audit reports for any questions on report format, etc.

Always keep the company informed of the audit results and what you plan to do from the beginning of the audit. No surprises. Determine if they will agree with the findings. Hopefully, they will which will make your life easier.

Also, remember to keep in touch with your requestor/customer during the course of your audit. Coordinate with them if you need their help. Also, get their agreement on any audit findings you may have.

Chapter 7

Meditation/Martial Arts Philosophy

An important thing to remember as an auditor is to relax. In a fight, the more adrenaline you use, the more tired you will get. Also, if you don't breathe through your nose, you will soon be out of breath. Try to relax and breathe properly through your nose. Move and react to your adversary. Always, keep your hands up to block. If you stand still and freeze, you may not make it out alive. If you can escape the first onslaught, see If you can connect with him and control him by connecting to his spine to control his movements.

By connection, I mean you have to actually touch your adversary which means you have to get close to him/her and stay in contract with their body so that you can know your adversary. Conserve your energy and you will have a chance to overtake your adversary at the right time. Practice sparring/fighting in real time conditions. Always see the whole body of your opponent. Do not concentrate on parts of the body as this may distract you. If you see the whole body, the slightest move can be neutralized, especially if your opponent has a weapon. If you attack, move at an angle to give yourself an advantage where you can hit your opponent but he can't hit you. Either cross and move to your opponent's left side or right side or straight into your opponent's space to crowd him so he can't clock you with either a right or left punch. This will prepare you for an attack on the street.

I was r recently reminded of the importance of planning and strategy when I watched a UFC fight on ESPN. There was a fighter who specialized in boxing and another fighter who specialized in Jiu Jitsu but was known for his punching power as well. It was apparent from the beginning that the boxer had really planned for the fight and had visualized what the Jiu Jitsu/power puncher was going to do during the fight. The boxer negated the opponent's strength by using his jab and moving backwards every time the Jiu Jitsu/power puncher went inside to try to hit him with a right hand. The boxer would also kick the Jiu Jitsu/power puncher in the front leg to sap his energy. In the last two minutes of the fight, the boxer took the Jiu Jitsu/power puncher's back so that he could not try a knockout punch. The Jiu Jitsu/power puncher looked completely over-classed by the boxer, because the boxer had negated his strength (power punching and grappling) by using the jab and kicks and capitalized on his weaknesses (lack of speed and strategy). This took tremendous planning and strategy to avoid/negate the opponent's strength and exploit his weaknesses. Try to carry this image to compliance auditing.

I highly recommend that when you look for a way to defend yourself by taking up martial arts, look only at masters who offer sparring/fighting. This is the only way you will ever get any good at martial arts. This is one of the main tenets of internal marital arts. A fight is like a marathon. You must make it through the beginning which is the most difficult part. You must be able to pace yourself and conserve energy. In Jiu Jitsu, they say if you get tired, you won't survive! Find the adversary's weakness. Move and find your opportunity with your hands up to protect your head.

Like martial arts, think of auditing as a marathon. Try not to burn out your brain as brain juice is limited. If you use too much when you are young you will be deficient when you are old. This is based on Taoist sex practices. Conserve your brain by working smarter instead of harder. Reviewing tremendous details and taking large samples will use a lot of energy versus having a clear objective, audit program, risk assessment, POER, sample selection based on risks identified. Simplify your audit and in turn simplify your life. The less complicated the better.

The Taoist philosophy is to conserve your sexual energy; otherwise, you may burn out and live a much shorter life if you use up your vital energy. Auditing is like a marathon in that there will always be more audits in your future. Take the audits one at a time and concentrate on what is important, identifying LOR and non-compliances. Make sure you organize your audit so that the peer review and supervisory review will go smoothly without a lot of comments. Write your report in a direct, simple style that gets to the point. These methods will simplify your life. To be successful at auditing is like martial arts, you must perform audits! Reviewing other people's audits, or working as a computer specialist, or other administrative job like policy making will not improve your skills as an auditor much. The only way to become a good compliance auditor is to perform audits! There is no other way.

Breathing/Relaxation. Breathe through your nose and inflate your stomach like a balloon. Learn pacing. Audit at a relaxed pace based on the circumstances.

Martial Arts – As a martial arts practitioner for over 45 years. I would recommend the arts of Tai Chi, Ba qua, and Jiu Jitsu. I recommend Tai Chi, Ba qua because of their philosophy of using an adversary's strength against him. Attack his weak points by making the adversary off balance. Don't use strength or force. Use the mind and follow the adversary. Throughout this book, I have tried to incorporate some of the teachings of Tai Chi and other internal arts. An ounce of strength can topple a 200-pound man if you attack first at the right moment and you can feel his energy by connecting with him. I have only been able to really "connect" with an adversary a few times while doing Tai Chi push hands. But with just a movement of my waist, I could send my Tai Chi partner 6 to 8 feet.

If someone could do this consistently, they would be a truly formidable adversary. In Tai Chi, you must be firmly rooted to the ground and your adversary will feel he is leaning against nothingness. That way he can't touch you in a meaningful way. This is the way of Chinese internal martial arts! Ba Qua uses the same techniques but I like the striking aspects of the arts. There are eight strikes used primarily.

In Ba Qua, you learn to hide your power by generating power from tensing your back muscles and spine. You basically become like a top! Your adversary does not know where your power is coming from. I used to practice with a forty-pound sword that was over 5 feet tall. A strike from an experienced Ba Qua practitioner would be quite devastating.

I also recommend learning Jiu Jitsu because it is really the only martial art (other than MMA) that allows you to "roll" with your adversary. Look for a Jiu Jitsu place that has no holds bar rolling and you will learn more in a few months than you would in a few years doing choreographed training routines. When someone is choking you out, you have no time to think. React! Find a way out. Jiu Jitsu is also similar to internal martial arts in that you are taught not to use strength. Instead use leverage to tire out your adversary. Control his hips, shoulders, neck, head, etc. This is similar to Tai Chi concepts, separate the shoulder or the hip from the rest of the body to weaken the adversary. That should help you.

A combination of these two martial arts would present quite a challenge to other martial arts or even if you are attacked in the street. At least you would have some practical fighting experience. However, most Tai Chi classes have been completely watered down to senior citizen exercise classes.

Find a Tai Chi/Ba Qua teacher willing to teach you push hands and sparring. These are pretty rare these days due to liability and the fact that most teachers don't want to teach real martial arts and many do not know the martial aspects of the martial arts themselves as they have never been in a real fight. You should have better luck at a Jiu Jitsu dojo. There is nothing like real contact no holds bar to train a person to expect the unexpected and how to react to extreme stress and anxiety. If you are attacked on the street there is only reaction and further action. Any thinking about anything other than the moment will usually lead to defeat. Your sole purpose should be to try to connect with your adversary and control his spine if at all possible. Move to the sides and don't play to your adversary's strengths. Maybe he's great at boxing but not so great on the ground or wrestling. Make sure to breath and relax to the extent possible.

Chapter 8
Conclusion/Phil's Inspirational Quotes

I would like to bring compliance audit out of the shadows and into the important position that it should be as an equivalent in importance to a financial audit. In these times of tremendous budget deficits, the revenue of this country can be used for great things or to reduce the deficit. I hope that I have contributed a little to this great country as the son of immigrant parents. I was able to get a public-school education here and developed the ability to write this book.

Even if you have no time to read all of this book, you can follow the concepts below which will surely improve your compliance audit in some way. You can always refer to these key concepts long after reading this book to reinforce what you are trying to accomplish as well.

The old kung fu masters would always improve or add martial art techniques and skills to what they already knew in order to create a better martial art. These styles were tested in actual combat. In auditing, you also need to meld different audit techniques and methodologies together to make your compliance auditing better. Use what works and discard what doesn't. Create your own Gung Fu audit style. This is what this book is about. Use finding LOR and non-compliances as the crucible of your fighting style and the measurement of your improvement and eventual mastery of compliance auditing. I have used my fighting style of compliance auditing to complete hundreds of compliance audits during my career which resulted in tens of millions of dollars in cost savings/LOR to the federal government. I have been considered the "Dirty Harry" of compliance auditing my whole federal career. Any dirty job that nobody wanted or couldn't complete was assigned to me. I do not have a perfect background to become a compliance auditor. I did not come from a family of professionals. My parents only had an elementary school education in

China and settled in Fresno, CA, a small town of only 200,000 people at that time back then. I was never recognized or promoted in 31 years in the federal government. I have been put down, ignored, and almost fired several times always toiling away in obscurity. In spite of this, I have worked tirelessly to improve my skills. I still have a giant chip on my shoulders! Rather than feeling sorry for myself and quietly quitting, this has led to me developing a new way of thinking and approaching compliance audits.

Management at Federal agencies who are in charge of supervising compliance audits need to train auditors earlier and in a more organized and complete way rather than giving various training on different topics over the years. My POER strategy is a combined beginning to end strategy which has proven results behind it. By teaching separate classes in a piecemeal way, focusing on certain trade areas or issues, you do not know if the auditors have a solid foundation when they start auditing in terms of planning and organizing a compliance audit. Training should be organized into all phases of an audit. This piecemeal approach leaves auditors forgetting about the classes they took right afterwards, unless whatever they are studying comes up in an audit they are working on currently. This is usually not the case and the training course is filed away and forgotten. Yes, most of my training courses were still in three-inch binders. Training the mind should be more of a focus and more emphasis on LOR and non-compliances rather than focusing on teaching the law and regulations with some examples and expecting auditors to develop a martial aspect to compliance auditing.

Reviewers of compliance audits at the management and supervisory level also need to focus on these areas to help auditors improve over their careers. Just dotting I's and crossing T's is not going to cut it, if federal agencies want to truly develop staff that can fight! A lot of audits are just posing with very little emphasis on results. Auditors can be satisfied with middling to no results without training. New auditors can easily get discouraged. Over time getting along with the auditee becomes easier if there are no findings and playing not to lose becomes easier. Playing the probabilities and gathering enough evidence to win becomes too difficult. It is much easier to lay off the auditee on difficult audits so they become more friendly and the audit becomes easier for the auditor to be liked. It is much more difficult to play the scientist seeking the formula for success. Especially when the company is not cooperative or fights against the auditor. Complacency will set in like rigor mortis. Auditing by rote and following what other auditors have done in the past become commonplace. Sometimes even copying what the auditor did previously.

I also recommend that audit managers and/or training coordinators make available to auditors the quality assurance checklists used by quality assurance audit teams. This way auditors will know whether they are complying with GAGAS requirements in planning, fieldwork, and reporting. It is better to uncover audits that do not comply with GAGAS before they are issued than after the fact. Remember, credibility is at a premium for compliance auditors. This will also give auditors a broader perspective of what it takes to put out a quality audit which involves all phases of an audit. Auditors can get this perspective easier if they are looking at it from the outside by being exposed to a headquarters team document.

Perhaps it is time that all these disparate compliance audit agencies at the federal level be put under the umbrella of a newly created Federal Agency/Oversight Board. With literally millions or even billions of dollars at stake, isn't it time that relevant agencies coordinate together and try to recover as much revenue for the government as possible! As our national security apparatus in this country has a budget of almost $1 trillion dollars and we imported approximately $2.5 trillion of goods in 2020 according to the U.S. Census, I believe substantial savings are possible if we just know where/how to look for them. This is a national security issue in my opinion. As the government can no longer raise taxes or cut spending, this is one of the few ways to increase revenue as President Biden is now increasing IRS staff in order to do just that. Maybe it is time for a newly created Federal Agency/Oversight Board to standardize, review, and track LOR for compliance audits so that they can be as efficient and effective as possible and collect the revenue that is due this country that we currently may not be collecting. This aspect of compliance auditing is being taken too lightly by the federal government and the public in a time of great need.

Also, as I stated in my Introduction Chapter, I am trying to build a respect for Asian culture and thinking. I believe this book could be a bridge that will help relations between Asians and other Americans in this country. We need to unify this country and the first step is for all of us to respect each other cultures and thinking. As Asians seem strange and foreign to other Americans, we as Asians need to bring Asian thought to the public; so that other races can understand us and know the brilliance of our culture

The examples I have presented throughout this book are for illustrative purposes only. I am only showing them to get you the reader to think. You need to take your brain out and wash it in the toilet. I am advocating a martial approach to compliance audits which requires knowing your adversary and finding his weaknesses. Following the money is the key, so reviewing payments is a must. What's the company's motivation? Do not blindly follow me, come up with your own way.

Some Key Concepts to Follow/Remember

To develop real auditing skills an auditor must be patient, objective, work independently, know his adversary, predict results to extent possible, be fully prepared, willing to take calculated risks, He/she must follow the audit program, agency guidance and GAGAS and be familiar enough with the regulations to be able to win audit positions. Even if there are no results to be found, as long as the auditor properly planned, organized, executed, and reported, then everything that could be done was done. Performing a complete audit with objectivity, sound judgements, a solid objective, and professionalism should be our goal.

We must also take the offensive as companies we audit have a lot more resources than the government which will be under more budgetary pressures in the future. We must work most efficiently and effectively within our means to get the desired results that we want for our agencies and taxpayers and ultimately to our country. We need to re-focus our efforts to build audit teams that can enforce government regulations and ensure the revenue for this great country. Anything short of that would be a shame. I believe it is time for a revolution in our way of thinking and performing compliance audits and I would like to be a part of this.

Be patient. Don't attack right away before you are ready. I have known many auditors who lost their credibility because they would claim the company, they were auditing was committing fraud without evidence right at the beginning of their audits. They later were proven wrong. This is the complete opposite of what you want to do. The only thing a compliance auditor has is his credibility and reputation. Once you lose that, you don't have anything, because nobody will take you seriously, the auditee, your management, and the customer. Observe the adversary. Analyze his strengths/weaknesses. Do your planning and training before the battle so you are prepared to attack when the time comes.

Don't attack the adversary's strengths, find and exploit his weaknesses. What does this mean in terms of compliance auditing? The auditee's strength is in his declared amounts for dutiable items, ADD/CVD, etc. list of excluded un-allowable expenses (DCAA). So where are the weaknesses. Try to find where the company has unreported or hidden items with potential LOR that were not disclosed to the government. Look for unreported high duty items, ADD/CVD, false FTA claims, related party, deductibility of NDCs, additional payments, assists, related party undervaluation, etc. not disclosed to the government. For DCAA look for additional unallowable or un-allocable costs in G/L trial balance based on nomenclature and value, allocability issues. Reasonableness issues as well.

Also, remember to use my POER methodology, as a connected audit is way stronger than an audit that is not connected. Putting it all together will make it a lot more difficult on the auditee as your planning documents, workpapers, evidence, and audit report will all be connected making the auditor a much stronger adversary. Remember to write the audit report for the customer to satisfy his needs. Your audit report should be persuasive with the goal of getting the auditee to agree to the findings.

What I am advocating for is something different. It is somewhat like developing a new martial art, in that I am taking ideas that work and integrating the ideas with other ideas to create something new and different. As I said, I don't have all the answers only that these methods/strategies have worked for me personally. I have actually "fought" in real audits for almost three decades and come up with really good results doing this. Of course, every auditor can modify and use whatever parts they feel are useful in this book. That is how martial arts is. You must adjust to every situation. In a no holds bar fight/attack, you must react, there is little time for thought, just rely on your training and ability to survive and get through.

Well, this is all folks! I have compiled 31 years of performing compliance audits into this book. Everything I know is in this book. I have held nothing back. My accomplishments are no small feat, even though they are completely forgotten today, I am still proud that I accomplished what I did on my own terms. The struggle goes on to be the very best that you can be. To get an opportunity to reach your potential. The few moments of reflection and happiness I got out of performing audits with great result were indeed fleeting. I hope to spread this around to the compliance audit community.

I end this book with a recommendation to US Customs Audit Management which hopefully will help this country fight the Fentanyl scourge as well as my contact information and a blurb about artificial intelligence. I love this country and hate to see it being torn apart by the rise of Fentanyl. This scourge on our nation must be dealt with somehow and I believe that US Customs can be the lead federal agency in this fight! We must cut off the money supply to these scum bags!

Recommendation: US Customs Audit Management and the US Customs Ports should consider taking the lead and/or offering their services to appropriate investigative agencies to identify importers involved in trade-based money laundering, especially from China and Mexico. As China is exporting ingredients to Mexico for the cartels there to produce Fentanyl and easily send it to the US,

This type of money laundering is usually accomplished by the seller/exporter grossly over-invoicing the value and/or quantity of the goods and the buyer/importer subsequently overpaying the seller based on the inflated invoice in order to transfer funds overseas (and sometimes vice-versa).

The Ports can utilize referrals from other federal agencies or identify importers that seem out of the ordinary (overstated) in terms of value declared to US Customs for review based on the value, classification, type of product, industry, country of export (China, Mexico), etc. I believe US Customs can also utilize artificial intelligence such as ChatGPT-4 to assist in these types of analyses.

I would then like to see US Customs Regulatory Audit (with the assistance of other specialists at the Port) more involved in identifying and auditing smaller importers who are most likely innocuously importing the goods at an inflated value and classifying the imports as duty free, to escape detection and payment of any duties. Through review of payment records/bank statements, auditors could identify who was paid (Chinese drug companies, known Mexican drug dealers) and where (China and Mexico) and they can ask why, for instance, a tourist shop would pay a Chinese drug company?

US Customs Regulatory Auditors can also request/subpoena the auditee's federal tax returns to correlate the auditee's business income to the dollar value of its importations/payments to identify potential excess money sent overseas. Any difference would be really apparent, especially, if the auditee's tax returns reflect the "real" business and not the inflated import/payment amounts. US Customs has the authority to obtain federal tax returns. The reason I know this is because on my last audit at the US Customs Field Office I worked at before transferring to the QA team, I assisted another Field Office on a financial capability audit. The Port requested the corporate and personal tax returns and, as a result, I identified millions of dollars that the auditee claimed he did not have but was forced to pay back to Uncle Sam.

Auditors can then provide assistance to other specialists at the Port to determine if imported goods are, in fact, grossly overvalued, and use: US Customs entry documents, appraisement of merchandise, inspections, payment information/bank statements, tax returns, analytical analyses, internal information, external information from other federal agencies, and any other evidence to support their position that the auditee is involved in trade-based money laundering. This must be a collaborative effort with US Customs and other cognizant federal agencies involved with trade-based money laundering.

Which federal agency could be more suitable than US Customs in identifying trade-based money laundering than the one that reviews transaction value and payments from the importer to the exporter? These foreign scum bags must be paid somehow and this is as good way as any to identify them! Going after the foreign drug companies/dealers with their assets overseas and monitoring wire transfers has not stopped this scourge. Sending US troops to Mexico would be insane! This is similar to my thoughts on reverse auditing. Why not try from the beginning (importer) to end (exporter) instead of end (exporter)! This is also following gung fu fighting philosophy, going from where we have strength (authority/information) over importers, instead of weakness (lack of authority/information) over exporters. US Customs has the authority to recover monies and even seize assets from parties (including importers) involved in illegal activities. I am unsure if the federal government has much (authority/information) over exporters. I know that the Department of Commerce goes after importers that sell to restricted parties overseas and to sanctioned countries. Perhaps US Customs and US Commerce can work arm in arm together on this!

But as I have explained before, that is the power of reviewing payment/bank statement information and another potential use for US Customs Regulatory audit, besides auditing for undervaluation, overpayment, and avoiding duties and fees! Just think of this as the opposite audit objective of overvaluation, overpayment, and avoiding duties and fees.

Regardless, we must stop this scourge on our nation by any means necessary! US Customs also needs to weed out the bad apples from the importing community who are running phony businesses in order to launder money overseas. So, this serves a dual purpose of helping to facilitate legitimate businesses!

As, I have not been involved in money laundering transactions, these are just the thoughts/musings of a retired auditor who cannot get hired in the audit field. I am being treated like a nobody even in my retirement!

A lot of times I have felt alone when I was performing my compliance audits. You are not alone! I will always be behind you in spirit! If your agency needs my help, I am available for speaking engagements as well as consulting or training roles. Please contact me at phillíphlee01@gmail.com, if you have any questions or would like me to speak to your audit staff.

If any of my readers find any errors or have suggestions for improvement for my book. You may also email me at: phillíphlee01@gmail.com

In addition, I am a great believer in ChatGPT-4 and artificial intelligence. I would love to work with software developers and auditors on creating an application for Compliance Auditing using Gung Fu Fighting Philosophy. I am hoping to use ChatGPT-4 to set up workpapers derived from audit programs and to act as a technical expert. If interested, you may also email me at: phillíphlee01@gmail.com

Inspirational Notes/Tip for success

- Focus on objectives LOR and noncompliance go hand in hand
- Planning is key. Properly plan your audit. Remember "Battles are won or lost before the first shot is fired."
- Connectedness of initial planning, audit program, workpapers, risk assessment, internal controls, audit report, hyperlinks and referencing to each document
- Materiality based on significant LOR, non-compliances with government regulations
- POER – Plan, organize, execute, report
- Procrastination is anathema to me. Avoid at all costs. Always try your best and give your all to improve your skills as an auditor
- When your supervisor/manager tells you to do something, do it right away to earn trust and make their jobs easier
- Always follow the audit program which is the fulcrum of your audit and Supervisory guidance
- Objective scientific predictive
- Use all information from planning, interviews, checklists, financial information about company, submissions, disclosures, in order to get an idea of how the company can rip off the government or increase profits through some kind of obfuscation.
- Risk assessment is crucial. Use all information available to defend against auditee -know your adversary predict his moves/responses. Risk assessment is like blood, audit program is like fulcrum/foundation
- Most auditors are honest, upright people and frugal people but to do compliance audit must be able to think like an adversary who is trying to get paid. Auditor is at severe disadvantage because adversary knows and you do not know where the findings are. As most auditors are extremely frugal with their own finances, they may not understand the need/greed of the auditee to engage in profligate spending like buying a private jet, yacht, or expensive jewelry or art. You have to have a "street" mentality on how to

screw the "man" to get government benefits in order to get inside the auditee's head.

- Change based on situation not fixed method of fighting. If information comes up during checklist, interview, adjust audit program and risk assessment
- Follow the money, find out how the company is increasing profits, review bank statements at smaller companies to verify payments as there could be double set of books.
- Review of payments/bank statements is a solid step. You can tell who, where, why the money went which goes a long way when auditing. Also don't forget vendor analysis.
- Always stay in contact with auditee. Be open about your findings as you have nothing to fear. Always be honest and upright.
- Look at both reported and unreported in risk assessment. review costs for unallowable, un-allocable, and unreasonable costs (DCAA), additional payments, assists, NDCs, etc. (US Customs). Don't attack strength, search for weaknesses,
- Training should be done at beginning and use checklists, shortcuts, information should be provided to auditors using in a direct way simply showing what are the problems to look for.
- Always make use of agency training materials and outside materials (Customs Broker Training) as a lot of details and test questions will help understand audit areas.
- Reverse auditing if no leads/nothing else works or as a probe to obtain more information about company
- Don't forget reviewing internal controls
- Organize audits to become one, audit program referenced to workpapers, which are referenced to audit support, audit report is referenced back to workpapers, etc. connected body remain closed open adversary
- Use simple direct language on audit report, emphasize customer, requestor. Ensure you are in step with them at all times.
- Take writing classes in school to train writing thesis papers starting in high school and during your college years
- Attack weak spots not strong, when their hard your soft, separate shoulder, you are closed, open them

- Conserve your energy, Auditing is a marathon. Pace yourself and don't wear yourself out. Work efficiently instead of doing a lot of busy work. Focus on objectives LOR and noncompliance, then things will make more sense. Wearing yourself out only helps your adversary. Then he can wait you out and control you
- Shelve your ego, concentrate on objective scientific evidence
- Get to point where you can predict outcomes
- Cite specific government regulations and develop a good understanding of the government regulations in workpapers and report
- What is your endgame and what do you wish to achieve?
- Never give up
- Use any scrap of information to win
- Play to win
- Outthink adversary, play chess game at highest level with your adversary
- Even if you've been put down, ignore them and continue getting better
- Rejection only makes you stronger.
- Learn from your mistakes and improve your skills
- Take constructive criticisms and be humble
- Look for adversary weakness
- Doesn't matter where you came from, as long as you can perform at a high level
- Meld different things you learn together to keep improving your skills
- Be open to new ideas
- Risk is an auditor's business but it must be objective and fact based on numbers.
- Always remember that adversary is trying to increase profits by not paying taxes/duties and approach in this way.
- Attack when you have enough forces/documentation to support your position. Only pursue findings where you have high probability of success based on company response and the strength of the evidence.

- Be patient. Study the adversary. Look for opportunities to attack adversary. Build up to the point where you can tell a coherent story about what the auditee is doing to avoid paying taxes/duties
- Look where the company doesn't want you to look, this is usually related to their pocketbook.
- Don't forget Unreported values
- Always have a positive attitude and approach audits in the same professional scientific way
- Always be open and honest with your auditee. Get them to agree with your findings if you can. That will make your life a lot easier.
- Put all your requests to the company in writing and create a worksheet to keep track of requests and follow up on late requests.
- Nobody can teach how to audit, but I am trying to show a certain way or method of thinking and how to approach a compliance audit. I am hoping those of you who have been put down or ignored can use this to enrich their professional lives.
- Focus on customer needs in report address concerns, work with government requestor and technical personnel. Always remember to satisfy the customer!
- Incorporate what is useful, discard what is not
- Auditing at the highest level is like a chess match. Think five steps ahead of your adversary. Attack and counterattack.
- Do not live on an island. Anticipate your adversary's response to your audit report and prepare to defend by stating government regulations, LOR calculations correct, evidence strong, planning must be good. Raise your hands, always be ready to defend yourself. Customer requests must always be addressed.
- Plan for auditee's response to your audit findings. Be ready to defend your position with scientific objective reasoning and evidence
- An auditor's integrity is his greatest asset, don't ever lose this
- Don't bother your contact without an appointment. Only contact them when necessary. Always appear mysterious, efficient, and confident to your contact.

- Materiality related to LOR and non-compliances. This must be your focus. Non-compliances with little or no LOR not as important
- Use everything against adversary ACE, training courses, HQ guidance, Regulations, etc., prior audits, disclosures by company, etc., Customs Broker Courses
- Follow GAGAS standards. Independence, evidence sufficiency and appropriate, etc.
- Refer to GAO Yellow Book for audit report format if you have questions.
- Always cite a government regulation when citing a non-compliance
- Remain flexible not static, revise risk assessment and audit program based on interviews and checklists
- Conserve brain juice like Chi, auditing is a marathon. Don't waste your energy when young. Work smarter don't overthink limited
- Always take a scientific, objective approach to auditing. Predict based on evidence is highest level. Obtain sufficient, competent evidence to back up your findings.
- Always consider customer needs. On requested audits coordinate and agree on objectives. On report get agreement with any significant findings.
- The only way to become good at auditing and marital arts is to actually practice and do it! This is the only way you can improve your skills by going out every day and fighting!
- Sampling plan based on risk assessment and internal control review.
- Always be diligent in your compliance audit work. Once information comes in from the company, immediately incorporate it into your audit. Don't procrastinate or be lazy. Run north-south. Focus goes from A to Z.

About the Author

Phillip H. Lee was born in Fresno, CA to immigrant parents from China who only received an elementary school education because of WWII. His father was an American citizen who returned to China as a baby. He graduated Magna Cum Laude with a B.S. in Accounting from California State University, Fresno, and is a CPA (Retired). Mr. Lee has performed hundreds of compliance audits during his career which resulted in tens of millions of dollars in cost savings to the federal government. He has 13 years of experience auditing at DCAA and 18 years performing audits at US Customs Regulatory Audit Division (RAD). His last two years at RAD were on the Quality Assurance Team. He retired from Federal service in 2018. He is currently employed as a substitute high school teacher in the Sequoia Union High School District. He is available for speaking engagements for anything related to government compliance audits or auditing in general.

www.ingramcontent.com/pod-product-compliance
Lightning Source LLC
LaVergne TN
LVHW090405210926
848480LV00002B/461
* 9 7 9 8 2 2 3 1 0 4 4 1 4 *